HOW TO DOMINATE THE PROPHETIC REALM

ANTOINE M. JASMINE

HOW TO

DOMINATE

THE PROPHETIC

REALM

HOW TO DOMINATE THE PROPHETIC REALM

HOW TO

DOMINATE

THE PROPHETIC

REALM

ANTOINE M. JASMINE

Self- Publishing Company, LuLu.com
http://www.lulu.com

How to Dominate The Prophetic Realm
Copyright © 2013 by Antoine M. Jasmine

All scriptures are taken from the King James Version (KJV) of the Bible unless otherwise denoted.

Scriptures noted NKJV are from the Holy Bible: NEW KING JAMES VERSION copyright 1982 by Thomas Nelson, Inc. Used by permission. All Rights reserved.

ISBN-13: 978-0692496787
ISBN-10: 0692496785

Printed in the United States of America

Library of Congress – Catalogued in Publication Data

Published by:
Jabez Books
A Division of Clark's Consultant Group
www.jabezbooks.com
www.clarksconsultantgroup.com

Jabez Books

1. Prophetic Insight   2. The office of the Prophet
3. Prophetic Terminology

DEDICATION

This book is dedicated to all the prophets, mentors,

teachers and pastors who labor in the prophetic. I

pray this manuscript will assist you in

the facilitation of the prophetic realm,

gift and mantle.

HOW TO DOMINATE THE PROPHETIC REALM

ANTOINE M. JASMINE

CONTENTS

HOW TO DOMINATE THE PROPHETIC REALM

ACKNOWLEDGEMENTS

I would like to acknowledge Bishop Joseph B. Hargo,

who has been extremely instrumental and

most influential regarding my life and

my walk in the prophetic; much

love to you, Bishop!

HOW TO DOMINATE THE PROPHETIC REALM

INTRODUCTION

In previous times God spoke through
his servants the prophets. It was abnormal
for any king during his reign not to be in direct
connection with a Prophet, and not to seek
the prophets of God in decision making. Today,
the prophetic ministry is very visible as God
promised to pour out His Spirit on all flesh and
have sons as well as daughters prophesy. The
gift of the prophetic is so refined; and as a
result, people are both interested and
alarmed by this dispensation. Prophets are
both feared and embraced. Those who
gravitate toward a genuine prophet receive
incessant exhortation, edification and
comforting; while others who are
apprehensive regarding the prophetic avoid
the prophet at all cost resulting in a loss of
manifold divine blessings. In times past,
prophets have been gravely

misappropriated as fortune tellers or soothsayers, and this compendium will provide spiritual guidance on the validity of the prophetic, the prophet(ess), and how to tap into and dominate the prophetic realm.

When prophesying, the prophet's ultimate focus is not geared toward individual, personal benefits for the person receiving the divine prophecy, but it is to build God's kingdom and allow the body of Christ to become more effective. For truly in these end times, now more than ever, God is releasing His Word and manifesting His will through His prophets. Because of this fact, it is integral to God's plan that Christians be informed of the operation of this supernatural, sacred, ministry gift.

As Christians we understand and validate the fact that God desirously orchestrated the five-fold ministry gifts as seen in Ephesians 4:11 NKJV. The office of the prophet is one of the five-fold ministry gifts designed by Jesus Christ "for the perfecting of t he saints, for the work of the ministry, for the e difying of the body of Christ." Therefore, the prophet is God's Mouthpiece, and he speaks directly for God in order to bring His Word into the earth realm. The prophetic mantle rests over many of God's chosen people; however, just as one had to be taught and trained to operate in the prophetic in the bible, it is imperative that those who are called by God as prophets obtain proper, effective training today. The prophet must experience comprehensive, extensive training from God. Hence, only God can call and qualify one as a prophet.

This manuscript is an invaluable tool that provides wisdom and knowledge of the prophetic realm. It expounds upon the operation of the prophetic gift and it teaches individuals how to dominate the prophetic realm. If you are considering enrollment in a School of the Prophets or training dealing with the Prophetic Ministry, please read this book prior to attending. AMJ School of the

HOW TO DOMINATE THE PROPHETIC REALM

Prophets uses this book as the basis for its course of study. Subsequently, whether you decide to attend our School of the Prophets, another prophetic school or if you only wish to gain a more in depth understanding of the prophetic, this book will enlighten you; and if you apply yourself, it will allow you to dominate the prophetic!

FORWARD

Prophet Antoine M. Jasmine is the Pastoral Overseer of Choice International Family Outreach Worship Center in Dayton, Ohio and LaPlace, Louisiana. He is the spiritual son of Prophet Joseph Hargo of Houston, Texas who is the protégé of Apostle Richard D. Henton of Chicago, Illinois. The "Prophet" as he is also known, is a structured entrepreneur and philanthropist and is the CEO of Choice International School of Music and Performing Arts, Anwar Publishing and Choice Entertainment Group. He is a member of the Business Network International (BNI), River Region Chamber of Commerce and serves on the Board of Directors of the Jefferson United Faith-Based Collaborative. He has been recognized in the "Exceptional Magazine" for his work in the community and in the May/ June, September/October issues of "Promoting Purpose" Magazine and in the

March/April 2013 issue of "Fresh Oil Magazine."
Prophet Jasmine was also the lead male role of
the play entitled "What's A Woman To Do?"
written by Evangelist Valerie Hooks.

Prophet Jasmine fulfilled his call as a Prophet
during his adolescent years and forsook his
degree in Mortuary Science to pursue a degree
at Bethel Bible College with a concentration in
Old and New Testament Studies. From that
time forward, he pursued the call of God upon
his life and has been used by God to set many
souls free. The "Prophet" travels throughout
the country speaking life to those who are in
need of direction and who are spiritually and
emotionally dysfunctional. He has the innate,
God-given ability to see into the lives of all
with accuracy and precision and the "special"
giftedness to take men, women and youth that
others have given up on, speak life to them
and bring them into their destinies. Clearly,
Prophet Antoine Jasmine has a heart to reach
the world.

ANTOINE M. JASMINE

Prophet Antoine Jasmine is truly in a category all by himself; many have accredited him as a Phenomenon. I have watched it with my own eyes, the colossal amount of oil that God has poured out on him. If a human being is going to walk in the Office of the Prophet, he or she must procure certain skills, the kind that separates them from the most paramount of the prophetic. This fashions a unique release of power into the lives of people in general and it demands a God-like response. If you have ever come into the fellowship with the now, Master Prophet Antoine Jasmine, you have been privileged to nest in the syndicate of one of the greatest prophets of all time. One might ask the questions, "How can such a young man walk in such a powerful prophetic anointing? Why is there such a level of success in his ministry? Lastly, how did he access the position to take the gospel to the world?" The Bible clearly states that is it good for a man to bear the yoke in his youth. It also states that I call the young because they are strong. Lastly, a childlike faith pleases God. Here is the description in summary: He has pleased the Father and the blessings of the Lord that make rich and add no sorrow have descended on him causing him to walk in absolute power. The success that is associated with him is due to the purity in his lifestyle. A purity as bona fide as frankincense and myrrh. These oils produce an aroma that attracts the Holy Spirit. I have discovered that God is attracted to the Prophet and He has emptied out His favor on him beyond measure. The result of this is success and you see it in every aspect of his life: success in business, success in music, success in writing, success in the evangelical arenas and most of all success in the prophetic. Jasmine was such an open-minded student in the prophetic that he has now graduated to Master Prophet.

He has mastered the three (3) dimensions of prophetic ministry. The first dimension is hindsight, having the ability to look into the past and explain profoundly what an individual has gone through. The second dimension is insight. This is when the Master

Prophet visits the present situation and explains profoundly the positives and negatives; he gives instructions and directions. This concludes with a sense of peace and practical and revelatory understanding. He precisely identifies what an individual is going through. The third dimension is foresight; here the Master Prophet looks into the future of the person and helps them to understand what God is going to do. Although a word of knowledge is accessible in every prophetic dimension, you see it more in foresight prophecy. A word of knowledge is not always revelatory but in most cases it is practical. This is a word that ignites the faith and helps the individual receiving the prophetic word to believe. When the prophet operates in this aptitude he may call out a name or an address; perhaps he will call out your date of birth or your social security number. This is all attached to "a word of knowledge." Only a skilled prophet of God has the volume to walk in such an extraordinary gift. Prophet Antoine Jasmine is that Skilled Prophet.

As a pastor he feeds the sheep giving encouragement, enlightening their minds and increasing their levels of prosperity in every dimension. As a teacher he is a man of instruction, training, structure and equality. He maintains relationships with some of the most profound men and women of God in the world. His intent, bringing in intellectual and theological mindsets to help streamline the persons he pastors, Prophet Antoine Jasmine is skilled in Theology, Christology, Pneumatology, identifying that he is not just a man of revelation but also a man of education. He serves in CORE Ministries, Founder and Chief Prelate, Apostle Amos Horton Jr.; this organization covers over 307 churches in various parts of the world covering churches in the United States of America, the Bahamas, and Liberia Africa. Master Prophet Antoine Jasmine receives with open arms this massive responsibility of being the Master Prophet of this entire organization. Prophet Jasmine is also the personal prophet to the Chief Prelate, Apostle Amos Horton Jr., as well as the male leader of prophetic protocol. His name is recognized in many churches all over the world. If anyone has experienced Prophet Jasmine going forth in the gifts and callings on his life, he or she has only scratched the surface in witnessing what God does through the Master Prophet Antoine Jasmine.

Apostle Amos Horton Jr.
Founder and Chief Prelate of CORE Ministries

HOW TO DOMINATE THE PROPHETIC REALM

CHAPTER 1

EFFECTIVELY PREPARING
THE GROUNDS

As we begin this profound coursework, it is imperative that you prepare your heart to receive the engrafted Word of God. One notable thing is that you must not harbor any unforgiveness in your heart. Just as a farmer prepares the soil to receive seeds that will bring forth a harvest, you too must have a prepared soil (your heart).

Whether the farmer desires a bounteous crop or a fruitful orchard,

25

preparation of the grounds is required for productivity. And so it is true in the realm of the prophetic. The successfulness of the operation of the gift of prophecy is contingent on the effectual preparation of the spiritual grounds. This fact cannot be sufficiently expressed. There will not be any consistent or accurate prophecy without adequate preparation.

Preparation is "groundwork" that yields good fruit. The properly prepared ground will produce fruit (prophecy) that is "good, acceptable and perfect in the sight of God." It can be described as a spiritual farming, where the grounds of the spirit must be tilled prior to operating effectively in the prophetic. Being effective in the prophetic leads to accurately prophesying, which leads to domination in the prophetic realm.

WHERE ARE THE GROUNDS?

What did we say are the grounds that

must be readied or effectively prepared? These grounds are said to be your heart. Do you recall what God said to Samuel in 1 Samuel 16:7 KJV, "...for the Lord seeth not as man seeth: for man looketh on the outward appearance, but the Lord looketh on the heart." Man's heart is important to God and the grounds of the heart must be tilled to make them fit for use by God. Preparing the heart is so important that Proverbs 16:1 NKJV clearly denotes that the preparation of the heart in man is from the Lord. Please ask the Lord to prepare your heart; this step is very vital to being successful in the calling of the prophetic.

Because of the fact that Jeremiah affirms this truth that the heart is deceitful above all things, and desperately wicked (Jeremiah 17: 9-10 KJV), and that the Lord will search the heart and try the reins, even to give every man according to his ways, and according to the fruit of his doings, the reality is that there is no way to achieve a fruitful, productive ground without the love of Jesus in our hearts.

Subsequently, we must renounce each and everything in our lives that is not pleasing to God. The Word of God in Proverbs, which is the book of wisdom- wise sayings, elaborates on twenty (20) things that are an abomination to God. What does God mean when He calls something an abomination? The word "abomination" is defined as anything greatly disliked or hated.[1] Therefore, as we search our hearts we must be absolutely sure that none of these are prevalent in our lives.

Proverbs 3:32 KJV declares that the froward is abomination to the LORD· Also, in Proverbs 6:16 KJV it speaks of what the LORD hates. Let us examine these twenty things:[2]

1. The froward man (Prov. 3:32 and Prov. 11:20)

2. A proud look (Prov. 6:16-17)

3. A lying tongue (Prov. 6:17 and Prov. 12:22)

4. Hands that shed innocent blood (Prov. 6:17)

5. A wicked scheming heart (Prov. 6:18)

6. Feet quick to sin (Prov. 6:18)

7. A false witness that speaks lies (Prov. 6:19)

8. A sower of discord (Prov. 6:19)

9. Wickedness (Prov. 8:7)

10. A false balance (Prov. 11:1)

11. Sacrifice of the wicked (Prov. 15:8 and Prov. 21:27)

12. The way of the wicked (Prov. 15:9)

13. The thoughts of the wicked (Prov. 15:26)

14. The proud of heart (Prov. 16:5)

15. Justifying the wicked (Prov. 17:15)

16. Condemning the just (Prov. 17:15)

17. Divers weights (Prov. 20:10, 23)

18. Divers measures (Prov. 20:10)

19. Refusing to hear the law (Prov. 28:9)

20. Prayer of the rebel (Prov. 28:9)

Therefore, we now understand that God literally hates these things, thus they must not exist in our lives or in our hearts. Also, the Word of God instructs us not to be partakers of other men's sins (1 Timothy 5:22 KJV). We must keep ourselves pure. So, it is important to the gift, the flow and the proper operation of the prophetic that our hearts remain "good ground," because any of t hese actions mentioned above can and will hinder the gift of prophecy, which is hearing God's thoughts and His voice.

THREE DIFFERENT SPIRITS

It is extremely imperative that we walk in the right spirit, which is the Spirit of God. In 1 Corinthians 2:10-16 KJV it tells us that God has revealed His secrets to us by His Spirit. God's Spirit searches all things, yea, the deep t hings of God. "*For what man knoweth the things of a man save the spirit of man which is in him? Even so the things of God knoweth no man, but the Spirit of God. Now we have received, not the spirit of the world, but the spirit which is of God; that we might know the things that are freely given to us of God. Which things also we speak, not in the words which man's wisdom teacheth, but which the Holy Ghost teacheth; comparing spiritual things with spiritual. But the natural man receiveth not the things of the Spirit of God: for they are foolishness unto him: neither can he know them, because they are spiritually discerned. But he that is spiritual judgeth all things, yet he himself is judged of no man. For who hath known the mind of the Lord, that he may instruct him? But we have the mind of Christ."*

Therefore, if the spirit of man or the spirit of the world is in us, we are carnally minded, and we cannot discern spiritual things. We must be spiritually minded and have the mind of Christ to know the things freely given to us by God, Our Father. Renewing our mind and taking on the mind of Christ is the answer. If we walk in the world's ways or the world's wisdom, we are not able to spiritually discern Godly, spiritual things. We cannot know or understand the things of God. If we walk in our own finite wisdom, we walk against God's wisdom and we will not be able to know the spiritual things of God. Only when our hearts are pure and we love God out of a pure heart will we be able to tap into the prophetic.

As we begin to keep our hearts pure and our hands clean, we will be able to hear God and know His secrets. Once we learn how to enter the prophetic through walking with God and staying in His presence, we will be able to dominate this realm.

FRUIT OF THE SPIRIT

As this journey into the prophetic begins, and as we continue to prepare the ground in order to be effective and successful in this realm, it is vital to understand the fruit of the Spirit and how it relates to our relationship with God. The nine-fold fruit of the Spirit defines, to an extent, righteousness. The LAW condemns sin, and no law can condemn one who allows these nine-fold fruit to be prominent in their lives. The bible states that there is no law against such fruit operating in the life of a Christian (Gal. 5:23 KJV).

As Christians, we are now light in the Lord, so we must walk as children of light. For the fruit of the Spirit is in all goodness and righteousness and truth; proving what is acceptable unto the Lord (Eph. 5:8-10 KJV). We must discipline our minds to ONLY focus on things that are true, honest, just, pure, lovely, of good report, virtuous, praiseworthy according to Phil. 4:8 KJV. We have a mandate given by Jesus to only do those things Jesus taught; those things Jesus spoke; those things Jesus asked us to receive, and all the things Jesus did. Jesus promised us that if we obey the commands, the God of peace shall be with us (Phil. 4:9 KJV).

Since we understand that it is LIFE or DEATH for the prophetic when deciding to walk in the fruit of the Spirit, we must identify and define these nine-fold Fruit (Gal. 5:22-23):[3]

1. **Love**-Greek- *agape*- divine love. A strong, ardent, tender compassionate devotion to the well being of someone

2. **Joy**- Greek- *chara*- the emotional excitement, gladness, delight over blessings received or expected for self and for others

3. **Peace**- Greek- *eirene*- the state of quietness, rest, repose, harmony, order, and security in the midst of turmoil, strife and temptations

4. **Longsuffering**- Greek- *makrothumia*

patient endurance; to bear long with the frailties, offenses, injuries, and provocations of others, without murmuring, repining, or resentment

5. **Gentleness**- Greek- *chrestotes*- a disposition to be gentle, soft-spoken, kind, even-tempered, cultured, and refined in character and conduct

6. **Goodness**- Greek- *agathosune*- the state of being good, kind, virtuous, benevolent, generous, and God-like in life and conduct

7. **Faith**- Greek- *pistis*- the living, divinely implanted, acquired, and created principle of inward and wholehearted confidence, assurance, trust, and reliance in God and all that He says

8. **Meekness**- Greek- *praotes*- the disposition to be gentle, kind, indulgent, even balanced in tempers, and passions, and patient in suffering injuries without feeling spirit of revenge

9. **Temperance**- Greek- *enkrateia*- self-control; a moderation in the indulgence of the appetites and passions

The nine-fold fruit of the Spirit are essential for prophecy. These spiritual graces manifest the work of the Holy Spirit on the inside of us. These gifts must be in full operation in order to dominate and possess the realm of the prophetic. They empower us with supernatural dynamics so that miracles, signs, and wonders will manifest. The work of a prophet demands that the prophet walks continuously in the Spirit and unendingly deny the lustful, fleshly works of darkness in order to remain pure and see what God sees, hear what God speaks, and reiterate what God says. The Holy Spirit provides what is needed to prophesy, and a continuous, untainted connection between Him and the prophet allows this to occur. Please meditate on each of the nine-fold fruit and ensure that every one of them is operating and fully active inside you.

GIFTS OF THE SPIRIT

Now, concerning spiritual gifts, we are not to be ignorant. There are diversities of the gifts, but it is the same person, the Holy Spirit that gives these gifts. There are differences of administrations, which are services, ministries, and offices, yet they are all orchestrated by the same Lord Jesus Christ. Next, there are diversities of operations or workings, but the same God works in all of them. Here, we see the work of the Divine Trinity:

A. Spiritual gifts by the Holy Spirit

B. Administrations by Jesus Christ

C. Operations by God the Father

The nine (9) gifts expounded on in 1 Corinthians 12:4-11 KJV[4] are given to individuals according to the will of the Father. A person may possess anywhere from one (1) to all nine (9) gifts. These gifts, achievements, and abilities are inspired and brought to pass by the Divine Trinity. The visible manifestations would result in the visible healings, miracles, manifest prophecies, tongues, interpretations, and even giving forth wisdom, knowledge, and discernments of various kinds. God provides us with the gifts to allow us to profit and prosper in everything we do as Kingdom Builders building God's Kingdom. Allow me to delve into the nine (9) gifts:

1. **Word of Wisdom**- supernatural revelation, or insight into the divine will a nd purpose, showing how to solve any problem that may arise

Ex. Solomon and two harlots, 1 Kings 3:16-28

- o Jesus and Samaritan woman, Jn. 4:16-19
- o Jesus and Saul/Paul, Acts 26:16
- o Paul on the ship, Acts 27:21-25

2. **Word of Knowledge**- supernatural revelation of divine knowledge, or insight in the divine mind, will or plan; and also the plan of others that man could not know of himself

Ex. The boy Samuel, 1 Sam. 3:7-15

- o Ananias, Acts 9:11-12
- o Simon Peter to Jesus, Matt. 16:16
- o Peter to Ananias, Acts 5:3-4

3. **Faith**- supernatural ability to believe God without human doubt, unbelief, and reasoning

Ex. Ask for wisdom in faith, James 1:5-8

- o Faith a grain of mustard seed, Mt. 17:20
- o All things possible, Mk. 9:23; 11:22-24
- o Impossible to please God, Heb. 11:6
- o Jesus is author, Heb. 12:2

4. **Gifts of Healing**- supernatural power to

heal all manner of sickness without human aid or medicine

Ex. Lay hands on sick, Mark 16:18

- o Gifts of healing, 1 Cor. 12:9
- o Nothing shall hurt you, Luke 10:19
- o Jesus healed all, Mt. 4:23; 9:35
- o Greater works shall you do, Jn. 14:12

5. **Working of Miracles**- supernatural power to intervene in the ordinary course of nature and to counteract natural laws if necessary

Ex. Divers miracles, Heb. 2:4

- o Aaron's rod. Ex. 7:10-14
- o Elisha and widow, 2 Kings 4:2-7
- o Elisha and dead boy, 2 Kings 4:8-44

6. **Prophecy**- supernatural utterance in the native tongue. It is a miracle of divine utterance, not conceived by human thought or reasoning. It includes speaking unto men to edification, and exhortation and comfort.

Ex. He that prophesieth, 1 Cor. 14:3

- o God spoke by prophets, Acts 3:21
- o Agabus, Acts 11:28
- o Prophecy by holy men, 2 Pet. 1:21

7. **Discerning of Spirits**- a supernatural revelation or insight into the realm of spirits to detect them and their plans and to read the minds of man

Ex. Jesus knowing their thoughts, Mt. 9:4

- o Jesus knew what was in man, Jn. 2:25
- o Saul and Elymas, Acts 13:8-10
- o Warning to us, 1 Jn. 4:1-6

8. **Divers Kinds of Tongues**- Supernatural utterance in other languages which are not known to the speaker

Ex. Speak with another tongue, Isa. 28:11

- o Speak with new tongues, Mk. 16:17
- o Pentecost, Acts 2:4
- o Gentiles Holy Ghost, Acts 10:44-48
- o Unknown tongue, 1 Cor. 14:2

9. **Interpretation of Tongues**-

supernatural ability to interpret in the native tongue what is uttered in other languages not known by the one who interprets by the Spirit

Ex. 1 Cor. 12:10

- o 1 Cor. 14:5, 27-28
- o 1 Cor. 14:13-15
- o 1 Cor. 14:27-28

These gifts fall into three natural divisions:

1) Gifts of Revelation

    a. Word of Wisdom

    b. Word of Knowledge

    c. Discernment of Spirits

2) Gifts of Inspiration

    a. Prophecy

    b. Divers Kinds of Tongues

    c. Interpretation of Tongues

3) Gifts of Power

    a. Faith

    b. Healing

    c. Working of Miracles

God has emphasized the number nine (9)

in both the nine-fold fruit of the Spirit and in the nine gifts of the Spirit. The number nine is a very significant number. It is the last of the digits, and this marks the end, which is significant of the conclusion of the matter. The number nine (9) shows that the signification is judgment, especially divine judgment. This number denotes finality in divine things.[5]

The number nine (9) is used 49 times in the bible and portrays finality or divine completeness from the Lord. Jesus died at the ninth hour; this completed His physical life. His death was the beginning of the finishing of sin and Satan. So here we see the conclusion o f the matter is to allow the nine characteristics of the fruit of the Spirit and the nine gifts of the Spirit to be active inside us; this will allow for total understanding into our development of focus on dominating the prophetic.

WALKING IN THE SPIRIT VERSUS WALKING IN THE FLESH

Before we can dominate the prophetic realm, we must identify and define the term "walking in the Spirit." Scripture tells us that if we choose to walk in the Spirit, we shall not fulfill the lust of the flesh, Gal. 5:16 KJV. Jesus taught us that the Spirit and the flesh are always warring against one another. Paul too was an advocate of this truth. As we walk with God we will be challenged and tempted by the things of the flesh- the lust of the eyes, the lust of the flesh, and the pride of life.

Jesus overcame all three of these fleshly temptations in the wilderness when He was tempted by the devil. He used the Word of God to combat the adversary. We must also follow Jesus' example and use the Word of God when in battle; there is no other way to defeat the enemy except by the Word of God. Walking in the Spirit is the continuous process of submitting your will to the Holy Spirit, so that Spiritual things prevail over carnal or fleshly things.

Romans 8:6 KJV tells us that if we are carnally minded death will be our portion, yet if we are Spiritually minded we shall have the fullness of life and peace. What is the actual definition of carnality? Carnality is defined, "pertaining to or characterized by the flesh or the body, its passions and appetites; sensual. I t means not spiritual; merely human; temporal; worldly."[6] Carnality is the total opposite of spirituality. It is walking in the flesh.

It is also important to understand that by our fruit, the things manifesting in our lives, we shall be identified. If we are carnally minded or fleshly, then the works of the flesh, which are denoted in Galatians 5:19-21 will be prevalent in our lives as opposed to the nine characteristics of the fruit of the Spirit and the nine gifts of the Spirit. What are these seventeen (17) works of the flesh:

HOW TO DOMINATE THE PROPHETIC REALM

I. **Adultery**- Gk. *moicheia*- unlawful
sexual relations between men and
women, single or married

II. **Fornication**- Gk. *porneia*- same as
above besides all manner of other
unlawful relations

III. **Uncleanness**- Gk. *akatharsia*-
whatever is opposite of purity;
including sodomy, homosexuality,
lesbianism, pederasty, beastiality,
and all other forms of sexual
perversion

IV. **Lasciviousness**- Gk. *aselgeia*-
licentiousness, lustfulness,
unchastity, and lewdness;
wantonness; and filthy lasciviousness
is the promoting or partaking of that
which tends to produce lewd emotions,
anything that tends to foster sex sin and
lust. That is why many worldly pleasures
have to be avoided by the Christian- so
that lasciviousness may not be
committed.

ANTOINE M. JASMINE

V.   **Idolatry**- Gk. *eidololatreia*-image-
     worship; idolatry includes anything on
     which affections are passionately set;
     extravagant admiration of the heart

VI. **Witchcraft**- Gk. *pharmakeia*- sorcery,
     practice of dealing with evil spirits;
     magical incantations and casting spells
     and charms upon one by means of days
     and potions of various kinds.
     Enchantments were used to inflict evil,
     pains, hatred, sufferings, and death, or
     to bring good, health, love and other
     blessings.

VII. **Hatred**- Gk. *echthra-enmity*-bitter
     dislike, abhorrence, malice, and ill-
     will against anyone; tendency to hold
     grudges against or be angry at someone

VIII. **Variance**- Gr. *eris*-dissensions, discord,
     quarreling, debating, and disputes

IX. **Emulations**- Gk. *zeloi*- envies,
     jealousies; striving to excel at the
     expense of another; seeking to surpass

and out do others; uncurbed rivalry spirit in religion, business, society, and other fields of endeavor; zeal; fervent mind; envy; jealousy; indignation and emulation

X.   **Wrath**- Gk. *thumos, wrath*- indignation; fierceness; turbulent passions; domestic and civil turmoils; rage; determined and lasting anger

XI.   **Strife**- Gk. *eritheia, strife*- contention; disputations; jangling; strife about words; angry contentions; contest for superiority or advantage; strenuous endeavor to equal or pay back in kind the wrongs done to one

XII.   **Seditions**- Gk. *dichostasis, divisions, seditions*-parties and factions, popular disorder; stirring up strife in religion, government, home, or any other place

XIII.   **Heresies**- Gk. hairesis- a choosing, hence a sect and heresy. True Christians apply this word to all false religions who do not accept the true

Christian doctrines. Heresies are opinions or doctrines contrary to church dogma; dissent or deviation from a dominant theory, opinion, or practice: an opinion, doctrine, or practice contrary to the truth or to generally accepted beliefs or standards

XIV. **Envyings**- Gk. *phthonol*- pain, ill-will, and at the good fortune or blessing of another; the most base of all degrading and disgraceful passions

XV. **Murders**- Gk. *phonoi*- to kill; to spoil or mar the happiness of another; hatred

XVI. **Drunkeness**- Gk. *methai*- living intoxicated; a slave to drink; drinking bouts

XVII. **Revelings**- Gk. *komoi*- rioting; lascivious and boisterous feastings, with obscene music, and other sinful activities; pleasures; carousing

The bible clearly and repeatedly tells us

that any persons who do such things mentioned above, these works of the flesh, shall not inherit the kingdom of God. It is vital that we denounce the works of the flesh daily and unendingly to allow us the ability to successfully dwell in the Spirit. A pure spirit is very fundamental and significant in the flow of the prophetic.

Once we begin to follow after Godliness and die to selfish flesh, we can build our character to resemble God's character. Also, we can have a pure heart and walk in integrity. The scripture admonishes us to "keep your heart with all diligence; for out of it are the issues of life," (Prov. 4:23 KJV). Our hearts must be pure and holy. God tells us to be holy because He is holy, and without holiness no man shall see the Lord.

In Psalm 24:3-4 KJV it states, "Who shall ascend into the hill of the Lord? Or who shall stand in His holy place? He that hath clean hands and a pure heart; who hath not lifted up his soul unto vanity, nor sworn deceitfully." When our hearts are pure, we can hear God clearly. The Spirit of God, living inside of us, guides our actions and leads us into all truth.

Now, the spirit man has been prepared and it is time to walk in the Spirit in order to move to the next level of understanding and to move into dominating the prophetic. God is always speaking, but we must be a willing vessel with a pure heart to hear and respond to His voice. Now that we have effectively prepared the foundation, which is our heart, we can move forward.

HOW TO DOMINATE THE PROPHETIC REALM

CHAPTER 2

PROPHETIC TERMINOLOGY

We, as Christians, know and believe that life and death are in the power of our tongue. Since the creation, found in the book of Genesis, we have learned that we can speak things into the atmosphere just as our Father, Jehovah Elohim, the Eternal Creator did. We have the power to call things that be not as though they were. In the prophetic, words are very important and the **power** possessed by the prophet should not be taken lightly.

53

For example, Elijah the prophet called
fire down to consume a captain and his fifty
men (2 Kings 1:10 KJV), and fire came
down! Elisha cursed in the Name of the Lord
the 42 little children that mocked him
(2 Kings 2:24KJV). Two she-bears came out
and tore them to pieces.

Prophetic words are very serious
and very important and should never be
taken lightly. The realm of the prophetic
is a spiritual, supernatural and vocal realm.
It is essential that we speak exactly what God
tells us to speak and not deviate. Scripture is
very important in prophecy. God is His Word, s
o He may speak a scripture or verse to
encourage His people. We must always be
sensitive to His voice and His supernatural
gifts of the Spirit, such as Words of Wisdom
and Words of Knowledge.

WHAT IS A PROPHET?

A prophet is a man or woman of God to
whom Christ has given the ascension gift of

"prophet."The woman is usually referred to as "prophetess." In this manuscript we will always reference **the prophet** but keep in mind that we are speaking of both male and female. The prophet is one of the fivefold gifts that is an extension of Christ's ministry to the Church, (Rambally, 2013).[7] He or she is an anointed minister who possesses the gifted ability to perceive and speak the specific mind of Christ to individuals, churches, businesses and nations. The word from the Greek translates, "a foreteller; an inspired speaker; a proclaimer of a divine message." In the Septuagint, it is the translation of the word *roeh*- a seer- indicating that the prophet was one who had immediate intercourse with God (1 Sam. 9:9). It is also the translation of the word *nabhi,* meaning "one in whom the message of God springs forth" or "one to whom anything is secretly communicated," (Rambally, 2013).[8]

The word *prophetes* means "to speak

before" or "to speak for." Thus it refers to one who speaks for God or Christ. Prophets were also referred to as "pneumatics" also *pneumatikos,* "spiritual ones." The prophet functions:

- ❖ To speak by divine inspiration or as the interpreter through whom the will of God is expressed
- ❖ As one who is gifted with profound moral insight and exceptional power of expression
- ❖ As a seer in spiritual matters because of what they see with their spiritual eyes in the spiritual realm
- ❖ To fortell future events and occurrences

Prophets have the strongest utterance because they speak by the Spirit of prophecy, the gift of prophecy, and out of the strength of the prophet's office, (Scott, 2013).[9] The testimony of Jesus is the spirit of prophecy, (Rev. 19:10 KJV). As we worship God with a pure heart in the spirit of truth, the Spirit of prophecy manifest in our midst. In Amos 3:7 KJV it states, "Surely the LORD God will do nothing, but He revealeth His secret unto His servants the prophets." A prophet hears the word of the Lord. In Jeremiah 1:4, 5 KJV it states, "Then the Word of the Lord came unto me, saying, Before I formed thee in the belly I knew thee; and before thou camest forth out of the womb I sanctified thee, and I o rdained thee a prophet unto the nations."

A prophet is approved by God; set apart or sanctified by God; ordained or commissioned by God. The office of the prophet is the only office that one can be born into as opposed to the other offices of the fivefold ministry. A person operating in the office of a prophet must be able to communicate the purpose of the Lord to the church. The spirit of prophecy is whatever you hear from the Father that gives testimony to Jesus..."...for the testimony of Jesus is the spirit of prophecy," (Rev. 19:10b).

WHAT IS THE PROPHETIC REALM?

The prophetic realm is the spiritual, supernatural realm from which God operates. God is a Spirit Being and only functions spiritually. This <u>realm</u> is the supernatural, spiritual place of authority by which God speaks through His servants. The prophet may fully access his authority and operate in this prophetic realm. The supernatural is the very essence of prophetic ministry.

The word "realm" is defined as: a domain in which something is dominant; the domain ruled by a king or queen; territory over which rule or control is exercised; a community or territory over which a sovereign rules; a kingdom; a field, sphere or province (Dictionary.com, 2013).[10]

The prophets are called the eyes; they function as the eyes of the Body of Christ. They provide vision so the church may go forward without stumbling. In Luke 11:34 KJV it states, "The light of the body is the eye:

therefore when thine eye is single, thy whole body is also full of light; but when thine eye is evil, thy body is also full of darkness. If we are going to function as the eyes of the body, we must be careful in how we use our own eyes.

Job exhibited great wisdom in that he stated he could not look upon a virgin, because he was in covenant (with his eyes) with God (Job 31:1 KJV). If our eyes are single, fixed upon the Lord, our entire body will be full of light. To be prophetic we must have the eyes of our hearts opened, not the eyes of our minds. What we see in the spiritual realm must be more real to us than what we see in the natural realm.

Abraham, the Patriarch of Faith, saw into the future and lived by that vision as if it were present day reality. Jesus confirmed in John 8: 56 KJV, "Your father Abraham rejoiced to see My day; and he saw it and was glad." Abraham was living for the eternal realm not the temporary realm. If our spiritual eyes were opened we would see things differently than we do now. Prophetic vision requires seeing beyond the way things are now- seeing things just as God said- not as they appear to be in the present.

By Jesus' death, He rent the veil that had b een placed over our spiritual eyes through Adam's sin, restoring our ability to see in the spiritual realm. Attaining true spiritual knowledge and understanding is progressive. It does not happen all of a sudden; yet, as you tap into the spiritual, prophetic realm, the eyes of your spirit and understanding begin to gaze into the realms of God.

God created us with more than just our natural eyes. We were created with spiritual eyes and ears by God, our Spiritual Father, in order to see and hear things that are spiritually discerned. In Matthew 11:15 KJV Jesus asked that he who has ears let him hear. Jesus was calling people to open up their spiritual ears and hear what the Father was saying.

Also, when Elisha prayed that the Lord opened his servant's eyes he was not speaking of his natural eyes for they were already opened. 2 Kings 6:17 KJV states, "And Elisha prayed, and said, LORD, I pray thee, open his eyes, that he may see. And the LORD opened the eyes of the young man; and he saw..." Here, the young man saw spiritual things on earth. The prophetic realm is one where our spiritual eyes and ears are opened.

The Greek word *anablepo* literally means, "recovery of sight."[11] It was used when blind people in the Holy Writ, healed by Jesus, recovered their sight. When Jesus was with the multitude, the **fact** was that He did not have enough food to feed them; the disciples saw this too. However, Jesus saw the **TRUTH.** He **recovered His heavenly sight** or saw into the spiritual or prophetic realm, blessed the food and the miracle took place. This occurred more than once. Therefore, the p rophetic realm is the proper position or the indefinite region or expanse where God's voice is distinctively heard and where the prophet receives revelation.

WHAT IS PROPHECY?

Prophecy is an outflow of the nature and heart of God as revealed by the Holy Spirit. It is an inspired utterance of a prophet, viewed as a revelation of divine will. Prophecy is a prediction of the future, made under divine inspiration; the vocation or condition of a prophet; a message of divine truth revealing God's will.[12] In prophecy the Word of the Lord flows and opens heaven to bring edification, exhortation and comfort.

Edification is "to build up." Exhortation is "to admonish or to warn." Comfort means "to console."[13] A prophetic word or the prophecy will be delivered according to the degree of faith that is in us, or to the degree of Word that is in us, because faith cometh by hearing the Word of God (Rom. 10:17 KJV). The level of your Word knowledge will also determine the strength of your word, and the level of the Scriptures will determine the type of prophetic flow that comes through you.

It is important to note that prophecy usually reinforces doctrine, reproves, corrects or instructs in righteousness. God is pouring out His Spirit on all flesh; therefore our sons and daughters shall prophesy. Whoever chooses to get into God's secret place shall receive prophecy: sight, hearing, illumination, revelation, strength and mysteries. "The preached Word is a sure Word of prophecy; God cannot lie!"

WHAT IS DOMINATING THE PROPHETIC REALM?

In Genesis, God gave man dominion over everything (Gen. 1:26 KJV). The word "dominion" is defined as: supreme authority; sovereignty; absolute ownership. It means: the acknowledged right to govern; actual control; a governed area; rule or power to rule; a governed territory or country.[14] Therefore, if we desire to dominate the prophetic, we must embrace our God-given power to rule and have supreme authority in the spiritual, prophetic realm. God has given us the acknowledged right to govern. He has placed His stamp of approval on us allowing us to have total dominion and authority in the spiritual, supernatural realm.

As I tap into my prophetic authority, God allows miracles, signs and wonders to be experienced throughout the service, the revival, the crusade or whatever arena in which God has positioned me. This is the place where God desires us to be--- totally **DOMINATING** the prophetic!

Another arena of dominating the prophetic is the empowerment to prosper. God said that He would open up the windows of heaven and pour you out a blessing- an empowerment to prosper- where you will not have room enough to receive. As a direct result of my prophetic gifting, and my ability to dominate the supernatural realm, God has blessed me with several supernatural creations that have transformed the lives of millions of people.

God gave me the directives to create several Blessed Oils; one is my Prophetic Connection Oil, and the other is my "I AM" Blessed Oil. My creativity has truly been sanctioned by God. These oils have been proven to heal the sick, raise a dead man and bring him back to life after 20 minutes, allow incurable diseases to be totally annihilated, allow people to tap into prophetic connections, not to mention myriads of other miracles!

I have just touched the surface of what God has for me while dominating the prophetic realm. God has provided us with the authority to do so, and so we shall move forward and successfully and seamlessly dominate the prophetic realm. Are you ready to dominate?

Let us move forward.

WHAT IS PROPHETIC REVELATION?

God desires us to get wisdom and understanding according to Proverbs. He loves us to communicate with Him, walk with Him and be in fellowship with Him daily. As we learn of Him (Who He is to us individually and intimately), He will begin to give us proper guidance, wisdom and instruction for our lives. Allow us to look at the relationship between God and Enoch. In Genesis 5:18 KJV, we see Jared begot Enoch, and after sixty-five years Enoch begot Methuselah and walked with God. In verses 23 and 24 of that same chapter we see "So all the days of Enoch were three hundred and sixty-five years. And Enoch walked with God; and he was not, for God took Him." Could you imagine awakening daily and having God in every area of your life on a daily basis? Can you wake up with God, perform your daily, personal hygiene routines with God, get dressed with God, eat with God, exercise with God, talk to God all the time about everything...can you imagine a life as such?

Enoch was born through the lineage of Seth and was the 7th from Adam. He was the only person besides Noah who was mentioned as being Godly in Seth's lineage, so we see that God can use any person He desires regardless of familial background. Jude 14 denotes the fact that Enoch was a prophet. He was translated by FAITH! God and Enoch had such a close relationship that God disclosed His plan for Enoch's life to Enoch, and Enoch selflessly complied. Enoch was taken to heaven *bodily* without dying. He was God's prophet of judgment who fought apostasy and idolatry while in earth, and he knew the time and purpose of his translation.

When we become so close in relationship with God that we NEED to hear from Him at all times, God will manifest His secrets to us. These secrets that come directly out of God's

mouth are known as Prophetic Revelation.
The Greek word *inspiration* that Paul used to
describe how the Bible was written literally
means "breathe out from God."[15]

We see in 2 Timothy 3:16 KJV that
all scripture is given by inspiration of God.
The Bible is God's revelation of Himself to us.
It is a book about God. Therefore, the Bible
is the revelation of God, Christ is the message
of the Bible, and the Holy Spirit is the author
of the Bible.

Prophetic Revelation is divine. This divine
revelation is different from other forms of
revelation. There are three (3) basic forms
of revelation: divine, demonic and human.
Divine revelation CANNOT lie! Divine
revelation is not rationalism; but rationalism
is human, carnally-minded revelation that
deceives with enough truth to make the lie
seem true when it is IN FACT not true!

Revelation is the process in which God
makes Himself, His Will and other information
known to mankind. The recipient of revelation

is commonly referred to as a prophet, hence, Prophetic Revelation.[16] God reveals His secrets to His servants the prophets. What God reveals to His TRUE prophets is divine, prophetic revelation. As you begin to serve God with a greater desire to know Him and to walk with God, He will commune or sup with you and Divine, Prophetic Revelation shall come forth.

We must understand that there are various levels of prophetic revelation. These range from mere impressions to being caught up into the third heaven like the Apostle Paul. Allow me to disclose the levels of prophetic revelation:

1. Impressions- the lowest levels of prophetic revelation that are put in our own words. These are incredibly useful when handled properly.

2. Visions- the next level of prophetic revelation, which range from those seen with the eyes of your heart to

open visions, which are like watching
a movie screen.

3. <u>Open Visions</u>- a higher form of
revelation; these are vivid and distinct
and are given in such a way that we can
not miss what the Lord is saying.

4. <u>Dreams</u>- a common form of revelation;
they can have different levels of clarity
and revelations. Some are bold and
direct, while others are gentle nudges
from the Lord. The dreams from the
Lord are easy to recognize as oppose
to impressions from our personal
activities or the food we ate, even if
we do not immediately know what they
mean.

5. <u>Trances</u>- these are the next highest form
of revelation, which are like having a
dream when you are awake; it is a vision
that is so real it seems as though you
are literally there, but you are wide
awake and aware of when you leave and
return.

6. <u>Directive Revelation</u>- Peter experienced a directive revelation in Acts 10. It was a vision to help overcome Peter's natural resistance that he should visit the Gentile household of Cornelius. It helped him make a critical decision and resulted in a major stronghold being brought down. We must have a clear understanding that prophetic revelation is not given to establish a doctrine; the Scriptures are given for that. However, prophetic revelation is used to illuminate doctrine or correct a wrong doctrine.

7. <u>Other Prophetic Experiences</u>- other high-level prophetic experiences include: hearing the audible voice of the Lord, being visited by angels, or being visited by the Lord Himself. Because now is the time of the great outpouring of the Holy Spirit, all of these experiences are becoming more common.[17]

HOW TO DOMINATE THE PROPHETIC REALM

CHAPTER 3

ENTERING THE HIGHER REALM

As we move into a higher realm, we must gain understanding of terminology with a greater level of spiritual insight. Allow me the opportunity to pour revelation into you. As this word is imparted in you, I declare that God will begin to open up your eyes so you may see; I use my faith to invoke your spiritual eyes to be opened just as Elisha prayed to the LORD for his young servant.

God desires us to be spiritually minded- more of a spiritual being than a fleshly being.

God says this and reiterates this all through His Word. We must enter into a higher realm of knowing God, a more intimate relationship with Our Father. Remember, we must be holy. In 1 Peter 1:16 KJV it states, "Be ye holy for I am Holy." Without holiness no man shall see the Lord. In Psalms it states, "*Who shall ascend into the hill of the LORD? Or who shall stand in His holy place? He that hath clean hands and a pure heart; who hath not lifted up his soul to vanity, nor sworn deceitfully,* (Psa. 24:3, 4 KJV)." God said, in Psalm 2:6 KJV, "Yet I have set my king upon my Holy hill of Zion."

When Zion is called upon, it refers to a higher place and realm in God. In the Old Testament Zion was the hill of Jerusalem on which the city of David was built. It was the citadel, a fortress or fortified place, of ancient Jerusalem. The word "Zion" also referred to Israel as the people of God. In the New Testament, the spiritual meaning of this word is God's spiritual kingdom, the heavenly

Jerusalem.[18] "But ye are come unto mount Sion, and unto the city of the living God, the heavenly Jerusalem, and to an innumerable company of angels," (Heb. 12:22 KJV).[19] There is a distinct relationship with Zion and the Prophetic and it is as follows:

1. Sight
2. Hearing
3. Illumination and Revelation
4. Strength
5. Release of Mysteries

In Amos 3:7, we understand that many mysteries are released in the realms of the prophetic; it is imperative that every believer know and understand that God always has **more to reveal**. Allow us to delve into some of the myriad mysteries of the Kingdom via scriptural references. First, we will elaborate on milk, meat and mysteries- the 3 M's.

MILK

1 Corinthians 3:1-2 KJV
And I, brethren, could not speak unto you as unto spiritual, but as unto carnal, even as unto babes in Christ. I have fed you with **milk**, and not with meat: for hitherto ye were not able to bear it, neither yet how are ye able.

Hebrews 5:12-13 KJV
For when the time ye ought to be teachers, ye have need that one teach you again which be the first principles of the oracles of God; and are become such as have need of **milk**, and not strong meat. For everyone that useth **milk** is unskillful in the word of righteousness: for he is a babe.

1 Peter 2:2 KJV
As newborn babes, desire the sincere **milk** of the Word, that ye may grow thereby.

MEAT

John 4:34 KJV

Jesus said unto them, My **meat** is to do the will of him that sent me, and to finish his work.

Hebrews 5:14 KJV

But strong **meat** belongeth to them that are of full age, even those who by reason of use have their senses exercised to discern both good and evil.

MYSTERY

Matthew 13:11 KJV

He answered and said unto them, Because it is given unto you to know the **mysteries** of the kingdom of heaven, but to them it is not given.

Luke 8:10 KJV

And he said, Unto you it is given to know the **mysteries** of the kingdom of God: but to others in parables; that seeing they might not see, and hearing they might not understand.

1 Corinthians 4:1 KJV

Let a man so account of us, as of the ministers of Christ, and stewards of the **mysteries** of God.

1 Corinthians 13:2 KJV

And though I have the gift of prophecy, and understand all **mysteries**, and all knowledge; and though I have all faith, so that I could remove mountains, and have not charity, I am nothing.

1 Corinthians 14:2 KJV

For he that speaketh in an unknown tongue speaketh not unto men, but unto God: for no man understandeth him; howbeit in the spirit he speaketh **mysteries**.

Ephesians 3:9 KJV

And to make all men see what is the fellowship of the **mystery**, which from the beginning of the world hath been hid in God, who created all things by Jesus Christ.

Colossians 4:3 KJV

Withal praying also for us, that God would open unto us a door of utterance, to speak the **mystery** of Christ, for which I am also in bonds.

1 Timothy 3:16 KJV

And without controversy great is the **mystery** of godliness: God was manifest in the flesh, justified in the Spirit, seen of angels, preached unto the Gentiles, believed on in the world, received up into glory.

Revelation 10:7 KJV

But in the days of the voice of the seventh

angel, when he shall begin to sound, the **mystery** of God should be finished, as he hath declared to his servants the prophets.

Mark 4:11 KJV
And he said unto them, Unto you it is given to know the **mystery** of the kingdom of God: but unto them that are without, all these things are done in parables.

1 Corinthians 2:7 KJV
But we speak the wisdom of God in a **mystery**, even the hidden wisdom, which God ordained before the world unto our glory.

Ephesians 1:9 KJV
Having made known unto us the **mystery** of His will, according to His good pleasure which He hath purposed in himself.

Romans 16:25-26 KJV
Now to him that is of power to stablish you

according to my gospel, and the preaching of
Jesus Christ, according to the revelation of the
mystery, which was kept secret since the
world began, but now is made manifest, and
by the scriptures of the prophets, according to
the commandment of the everlasting God,
made known to all nations for the obedience of
faith.

So we see that milk is for the novice
Christians, the babes in Christ; those who
have just come to Christendom. While meat
is for the seasoned Christians; those who are
knowledgeable in the things of God. However,
mysteries are for the more profound people
of God who are looking to Him and searching
His scriptures for more. They are actually
walking with God and conversing with Him. If
we are going to dominate the prophetic realm,
we must seek out the mysteries or the Greek
word *mysterion,* which literally means "to shut
the mouth."[20] The mystery is the revelation of
a secret that had not been known before and

one which is known only by a certain few and is kept hidden from all others.

THE PURPOSE OF MIRACLES

Does God still perform tangible miracles today? The answer to this question is a simplistic "yes." God is still in the miracle working business. The essence of a miracle defines Who is our Sovereign Master- Adonai Jehovah. Sixteen times in the Pentateuch, it is evident that the purpose of miracles was to cause all men to know that God is the ONLY TRUE and LIVING GOD. Many other times it is clear, without ambiguity, that God has done things to prove to men that He is God. No less than 75 times in Ezekiel alone are such statements found as, "They shall know that I am the Lord," (Dake's, 2010).[21]

Jesus said in John 14:12 KJV, "Verily, verily I say unto you, he that believeth on me, the works that I do shall he do also; and greater works than these shall he do; because I go unto my Father. So we see that each and every **believer** will do the works that Jesus did. In the Greek, the word *ergon* translates works, deeds and acts.[22] Subsequently, it is certain that Jesus was referring to miracles, healings, signs, wonders and mighty acts of power.

Jesus' works consisted of healing all manner of sickness and disease, cleansing lepers, casting out demons, raising the dead, and performing innumerable acts of deliverance from all the works of Satan. He controlled the elements, multiplied food, turned water into wine, walked on water, restored a severed ear, accomplishing anything He set out to do in the material and spiritual realms. Jesus commanded that the works He did shall all who believe on Him do just as He did. He also stated that these TRUE BELIEVERS shall accomplish greater works than all the works He had done while in earth in His incarnate state.

In verse 12 above, the word "shall"

denotes the fact that Jesus promised here
that each and every believer CAN BE endued
with power and receive the Spirit without
measure. Each believer can have equal power
with Christ to accomplish what He did and to
do greater things if and when the occasion
requires it. Allow me the opportunity to
elaborate on the fact that we will NOT have
greater power than Jesus, but we can emulate
His works and His power through this authority
He has given us in this passage of Scripture. W
e are authorized to do greater works, but
we do not have greater power. Remember,
Jesus is God and Psalms reminds us that all
power belongs to God. He is Omnipotent-
all powerful.

REASONS FOR GREATER WORKS IN DOMINATING THE PROPHETIC REALM

The true, valid and legitimate reasoning
behind our ability to perform greater works
than Jesus rests in the fact that Satan is cast
out (John 12:31). On the cross Jesus defeated

sin, death, the grave, hell and Satan. Jesus completed redemption, where WE now have TOTAL ability to be like Jesus through the Spirit of baptism, which could not be given until Jesus was glorified.

When Christ, our Redeemer, went back to the Father He promised us He would continue to intercede for us (Romans 8:34). Christ is the Headship of all powers and there is no name above the Name of Jesus. Therefore, all authority given to Christ was for Him to endow His believers with this same auspicious, dynamic, dynamite power in the AUTHORITY of His Name. The life, death and resurrection of Jesus allows every believer to enter into the holiest of holies.

Jesus gave His power to all His disciples and believers to carry on with power and continue where He left off. Jesus understood that we, on earth, have a time limit, so He mandated time for the universality of the program of God in blessing all nations. Jesus mandated time for the true believers to be fully equipped to do God's Kingdom building. Now is the TIME of no limitations in Christ, in the Spirit, and in the full benefits of all the gospel promises.

CHAPTER 4

THE THIRD HEAVEN

In Genesis 1:1 KJV it states that in the beginning God created the heaven and the earth. Also, Genesis 2:1 KJV states thus the heavens and the earth were finished, and all the host. Verse 4 states that these are the generations of the heavens and of the earth when they were created, in the day the Lord God made the earth and the heavens. In Psalm 102:25 KJV the bible declares, "Of old hast thou laid the foundation of the earth:

and the heavens are the work of thy hands."

There exist the heavens, which are a separate entity from the world, and the world which is a separate entity from the earth. Psalm 77:18 KJV states, "The voice of thy thunder was in the heaven: the lightnings lightened the world: the earth trembled and shook." In 2 Corinthians 12:1-4 KJV it states, *"It is not expedient for me doubtless to glory. I will come to visions and revelations of the Lord. I knew a man in Christ above fourteen years ago, (whether in the body, I cannot tell; or whether out of the body, I cannot tell: God knoweth;) such an one caught up to the third heaven. And I knew such a man, (whether in the body, or out of the body, I cannot tell: God knoweth;) How that he was caught up into paradise, and heard unspeakable words, which it is not lawful for a man to utter."*

The bible speaks of three (3) heavens. The first being our immediate atmosphere,

the second is outer space as far as it
stretches, and the third is the place where
God Himself dwells. Therefore, if there is a
third heaven we can conclude that there also m
ust be a first and second heaven as well.
God is a God of order. We are only
elaborating on the third heaven.

The third heaven is where God, the holy
angels (and creatures), and the Spirits of just
men dwell. It is also referred to as the heaven
of heavens. Let us take a look at several
scriptures:

Deut. 10:14 KJV- Behold, the heaven and the
heaven of heavens is the Lord's thy God, the
earth also, with all that therein is.

1 Kings 8:27 KJV- But will God indeed dwell
on the earth? behold, the heaven and
heaven of heavens cannot contain thee;

Psalm 155:16 KJV- the heaven, even the
heavens, are the Lord's: but the earth hath
He given to the children of men.

Psalm 148:4 KJV- Praise Him, ye heaven

of heavens, and ye waters that be above the heavens.

The third heaven is beyond the space and the stars. No man has ever seen this third heaven by telescope or in any other manner unless God revealed it to him (Paul). Hebrews 8:1 KJV states, Now of the things which we have spoken this is the sum: We have such an high priest, who is set on the right hand of the throne of the Majesty **in the heavens.** We also see that Christ called heaven His Father's house (John 14:2) and He also called it paradise (Luke 23:43). Heaven is the location of "The heavenly Jerusalem" before it comes to earth. The third heaven is the highest heaven where God is; the seat of the divine Majesty, and the residence of the holy angels; where the souls of departed saints go immediately upon their death; and the bodies and souls of those who have been translated, caught up, and raised already, are; and where the glorified body of Christ is and will be until his second coming.

The Apostle Paul had the exalted experience of being caught up in the third heaven and he received communications and revelations which he was not permitted to make known. Paul heard "unspeakable words, which it is not lawful for man to utter."[23] The word "revelation" means an uncovering. Paul had a cover removed and saw things of the third heaven as they are hid behind the veil. He could have had this experience in three different ways: a vision, caught up bodily into heaven, or separation of body and spirit, where his body remained in earth, while he traveled in spirit.

A vision is an experience where sight becomes supernatural just as the human eye would see things if they were physically there. Therefore, a vision corresponds exceptionally close to reality. Ephesians 1:3 KJV declares God has "blessed us with all spiritual blessings in heavenly places in Christ:"

So, now that we understand the position of the third heaven, the place where God dwells, we can reveal the fact that we must co-exist within the heavens always endeavoring to reach the third heaven in order to dominate the prophetic realm. Since God already desires us to be more of a spiritual being, here we understand the magnificence of God's reasoning for this. We must go higher and become as close to God as possible in order to operate in the realms of the Spirit.

SEEK THOSE THINGS THAT ARE ABOVE

In Ephesians we see that Jesus ascended u p far above all heavens. Subsequently, we are admonished, in Colossians, that if we are risen with Christ we must seek those things which are above. Our affection---which is fond attachment, devotion or love---, according to the Word of God, must be set on things above and not on earthly things. This means we are to love heavenly things and be engrossed by them. The word "engrossed" means to occupy completely, as the mind or attention; to absorb.[24] Because of this fact, it is so important that we continuously exhort one another. Perhaps we know TOO LITTLE of the glorious things above to love them heartily.

Because we are men and women of God, the impenetrable veil which covers the land of immoral beauty can be opened to us, yet ONLY because of God, through Him and at His will. As we begin to renew our minds with the Word of God, transform our thinking and put on the renewed mind of Christ, pray, meditate, and seek God's face wholeheartedly God's Spiritual Realm will be opened unto us. H ere, we can not only enter into the prophetic re alm but we can also dominate it as we move from faith to faith (Rom. 1:17), from strength t o strength (Psa. 84:7), from grace to grace (John 1:16), from glory to glory (2 Cor. 3:18) and grow brighter and brighter (Prov. 4:18).

THE SIGNIFICANCE IN THE NUMBER THREE

God is the Father; Jesus is the Son, and the Comforter is the Holy Spirit. Hence, as a result of these factors, we understand the spiritual importance, the miraculous importance and the gargantuan significance of the number three (3). The number three stands for that which is solid, real, substantial, complete, and entire. When we look into the Scriptures, this completeness becomes divine marking Divine completeness o r perfection. Three is the number of divinity.

Three is the number of resurrection. We first see this number in Genesis 1:13 KJV in the third day. This was the day the earth was caused to rise up out of the water, symbolic of that resurrection life which we have in Christ Jesus. It was also on the third day that Jesus rose again from the dead.
Jesus was crucified in the third hour; it was the first three (3) hours (from the 6th to

the 9th) that a shroud of darkness covered our Lord and Savior; it was the third day on which Jesus was perfected. While we are speaking of Divine perfections and the number three (3), let us note all of the dynamic examples of this number used by Christ and in His ministry while He was in the earth realm. Jesus raised three people from the dead. He was perfected i n office because He was the Prophet, the Priest and the King. The inscriptions on the cross in three languages reveal the completeness of His rejection by man. The temple is marked by three- three parts: the Court, the Holy Place and the Sanctuary. It also had three chambers around it.

The Old Testament is divided into three: the Law, the Prophets and the Psalms. There are three gifts of grace: Faith, Hope and Love. There are three temptations: the lust of the flesh, the lust of the eyes and the pride of life. There were three people who God told to ask Him of anything. There were three righteous

Patriarchs before the flood: Abel, Enoch and Noah. There were three righteous patriarchs after the flood: Abraham, Isaac and Jacob. There were three key apostles who witnessed Jesus' transfiguration: Peter, James and John. Jesus prayed three times in the Garden of Gethsemane. In the first chapter of the Book of Revelation- the revelation of Jesus Christ, almost every verse denotes Jesus in some three-fold relation. Three denotes divine perfection.

The third heaven is where God resides. It denotes the divine perfection of heaven, as well as divine perfection of everything. There exists nothing flawed in heaven; total perfection, total completeness; the essence of God!

CHAPTER 5

THE POWER OF A TRUE PROPHETIC CONNECTION

We have been inundated with so much information thus far and now we will begin disclosing knowledge about tapping into a true prophetic connection. We understand that the whole essence of the prophetic is to go to the original mind of God and the plan He had for our lives from the beginning. God created humanity with a plan and purpose, an agenda, for our lives. As we seek God for instruction it brings us to His prophetic destiny.

Many people today have deliberately and inadvertently abused the term "prophet." As a result, we must ensure that the prophet of God covering us is a true, untainted Man of God. The "prophetess" would be the Woman of God. Some people out of greed and ignorance have perverted the true power of the prophet, but God has given us foolproof methods to recognize true prophets and prophetesses from the false ones. If we follow God and His Word, we will not be deceived---God promised.

As we tap into the power of the connection to a true prophet/prophetess, we are referencing the office of the prophet and not merely the prophetic anointing. There is a distinct difference between the prophetic anointing and the office of the prophet. In 1 Corinthians 14:1, 3-5 NKJV it states, "Pursue love and desire spiritual gifts, but especially that you may prophesy. But he who prophesies speaks edification and exhortation and comfort to men. He who speaks in a

tongue edifies himself, but he who prophesies
edifies the church. I wish you all spoke with
tongues, but even more that you prophesied;
for he who prophesies is greater than he who
speaks with tongues, unless indeed he
interprets, that the church may receive
edification." 1 Corinthians 14:22, 24-25 NKJV s
ays, "Therefore tongues are for a sign, not to t
hose who believe but to unbelievers; but
prophesying is not for unbelievers but for
those who believe. But if all prophesy, and
an unbeliever or an uninformed person comes i
n, he is convinced by all. And thus the
secrets of his heart are revealed; and so,
falling down on his face, he will worship God
and report that God is truly among you." Also,
1 Corinthians 14:31-33 NKJV states, "For you c
an all prophesy one by one, that all may
learn and may be encouraged. And the spirits
of the prophets are subject to the prophets.
For God is not the author of confusion but of
peace, as in all the churches of the saints."

Subsequently, all may prophesy, but all are not called to the office of the prophet. **God chooses** who **He desires** to use as a PROPHET/ PROPHETESS.

The office of the prophet is run by a resident person referred to as a *Prophet* (a woman would be *Prophetess*). He/ She may be operating in a church or may have branched out to start his/her own ministry, yet this ministry is still run with a heavy prophetic base. So, the fundamental nature of the prophetic is to obtain God's desire for our lives. The original mind of God concerning our lives, the revelation of the future, any detours and the causes of those impediments, and the steps to get us back on track are all obtained through the power of the prophetic connection. God also corrects or chastens people through the prophetic. God speaks what is urgent or what is on His heart or His agenda for that day. It is time to bring back the sheer power and full nature of the prophetic.

It is a very severe and awesome

responsibility to give the unadulterated Word of the Lord. The virtue that comes out of the mouth of a prophet should NOT be taken lightly; neither is it a game! Deuteronomy 18: 18 KJV states, "I will raise them up a Prophet from among their brethren, like unto thee, and will put my words in his mouth; and he shall speak unto them all that I command him." Here, we understand it is God's will for us to have prophets in the earth. Since we all agree and are on one accord with this truth, allow us to move on.

There are numerous blessings that come with positioning oneself with a true prophet, hence a divine and true prophetic connection. We see in Hosea 12:13 KJV, "And by a prophet the LORD brought Israel out of Egypt, and by a prophet was he preserved." **A true prophetic connection brings one out of bondage.** Many people have been set free from the chains and yokes of bondage under my prophetic anointing. God has used my gift to touch many people all over the world; there are mounds and mounds of testimonies regarding people being fully delivered from their bondage. Families have been delivered from generational curses of bondage all through a true prophetic connection.

A true prophetic connection brings preservation. Not only does the power of the prophet and his divine connection between God and His people bring you out of bondage, but it brings preservation. 1 Kings 17:14-16 KJV states, *"For thus saith the LORD God of Israel, The barrel of meal shall not waste, neither shall the cruise of oil fail, until the day that the LORD sendeth rain upon the earth. And she went and did according to the saying of Elijah: and she, and he, and her house, did eat many days. And the barrel of meal wasted not, neither did the cruise of oil fail, according to the word of the LORD, which he spake by Elijah."* Obeying the words of the prophet brings preservation of life, food, finances, jobs, stability, family, relationships, etc.

A true prophetic connection releases mantles. A mantle is a cloak of divine authority. In the history of the bible, mantles, which were cloaks worn by God's anointed, were literally passed down from the prophet to his successor. Today, the prophet does not wear a literal cloak, but the mantle is still passed down; it is spiritual. Let us look at 1 Kings 19:19 KJV, *"So he departed thence, and found Elisha the son of Shaphat, who was plowing with twelve yoke of oxen before him, and he with the twelfth: and Elijah passed by him, and cast his mantle upon him."* The supernatural power of the prophet can be passed down to those God chooses to do His will. Many are called, but few are chosen.

2 Kings 2:12-14 KJV states, *"And Elisha saw it, and he cried, My father, my father, the Chariot of Israel, and the horsemen thereof. And he saw him no more: and he took hold of his own clothes, and rent them in two pieces. He took up also the mantle of Elijah that fell*

from him, and went back, and stood by the Bank of Jordan; And he took the mantle of Elijah that fell from him, and smote the waters, and said, Where is the LORD God of Elijah? And when he also had smitten the waters, they parted hither and thither: and Elisha went over."

A true prophetic connection releases inheritance. Elisha inherited a double portion of Elijah's spirit. Elisha could not have gotten this from his biological father, but because God had chosen him he received this blessing from God the Father through His servant the prophet, Elijah! Here we also notice once Elisha saw that Elijah's mantle had been left behind for him, he stripped off the old clothes to embrace the new cloak and all that came with inheriting it. **A true prophetic connection requires a stripping of the old and an embracing of the new.**

As Elisha followed Elijah for years and poured water in his hands as his servant, this serving caused him to be prepared for elevation. **A true prophetic connection prepares me for promotion.** The bible clearly tells us that promotion comes from above (Psa. 75:6-7 and James 4:10). There is nothing we can do to promote ourselves in God's kingdom, but in due season God will elevate His faithful. Serving God's prophet is a sure way to receive an expedited promotion.

A true prophetic connection is preparation for separation. Elisha began following and serving the Prophet of God, Elijah. As a result of this relationship, Elijah prepared Elisha for his departure and separation. God allows one to be trained for subsequent separation, elevation and promotion. **A true prophetic connection requires a "father" or a mentor (teacher).** In order for you to become great, you must serve greatness. In order for you to learn the things of God, you must be taught. In the Biblical days there were Schools of the Prophets. The students had to study and be

taught and mentored to walk in this office,
because **a true prophetic connection
releases power and authority.** Once
Elisha served Elijah the word was out. Because
of the powerful anointing on Elijah, Elisha
was also well known due to the relationship.
2 Kings 3:11 KJV states, *"But Jehoshaphat
said, Is there not here a prophet of the LORD,
that we may enquire of the LORD by him? And
one of the king of Israel's servants answered
and said, Here is Elisha the son of Shaphat,
which poured water on the hands of Elijah."*
**A true prophetic connection requires
servant hood.** As a result of the servitude
of Elisha to Elijah, his name and power was
also well known all the way up to the King.
Proverbs 18:16 KJV says that a man's gift will
make room for him, and bring him before
great men. We also know of Joseph and his
ability to interpret dreams, and many others
in the Holy Writ whose gifts introduced them
to greatness.

    A true prophetic connection releases

favor and prosperity. We can agree that favor can take you where money cannot. A person with a deadly disease can have all the money in the world, but if that sickness is to death he or she will leave that money here and die an untimely death. However, **a true prophetic connection can release the favor of God on a person's life** and allow them a miracle to live. Hezekiah is our example. His time to leave the earth came, and the angel of the Lord told him to get his house in order. He prayed to the Lord and reminded the Lord of how faithful he was, and the Lord provided him with an additional fifteen years to live. Let us look at Elisha's death. The Israelites were burying a man, but a raid was occurring, so they threw the corpse in Elisha's grave and when the corpse touched the bones of Elisha the man revived and stood up on his feet (2 Kings 13:21). The bones of the dead prophet still had power to resurrect a dead corpse---the true prophetic connection has supernatural benefits.

A true prophetic connection requires an upgrade, not a downgrade. John 13: 16 KJV states, *"Verily, verily, I say unto you, The servant is not greater than his lord; neither he that is sent greater than he that sent him."* Elijah was greater than Elisha, and Elisha received a divine, supernatural upgrade once his father left. Once a person comes into contact with a prophet, he or she will experience profound increase, overflow and favor. It is inevitable for an upgrade to occur.

These are some of the basic benefits of having a true prophetic connection. However, God is not limited so there are a myriad of benefits one acquires because of the relationship of the true prophetic connection. We cannot limit God in any way because with God all things are possible.

CHAPTER 6

THE POWER OF THE PROPHET

The prophet is God's spokesperson; he is God's mouth piece, which verbalizes God's Words as the Spirit directs. The Greek word *propheteia* means "speaking forth the mind and counsel of God and a voice of Christ in speaking to the Church."[25] This person has been chosen and called out by God and has been consecrated to carry the heart of God to the body of Christ. God establishes a special, elected being to minister words from Him to you. This is the assignment of the prophet:

edification, exhortation and comfort.

Jesus Christ, our Lord, both an Apostle and a Prophet, went through the greatest sufferings in order to obtain the keys to the Kingdom, so that we can receive and have what God wants to give us. Just as Jesus received the God-given reward of having dominion over the earth, a prophet will receive a reward for the price the prophet has paid and continues to pay because he carries the anointing.

Our time here in the earth is a narrow portion of the time spectrum in contrast to eternity forever. If we understand this theory along with light and our visual spectrum, we can gain more of an understanding of the things beyond the physical limitations of natural eyesight into the fascinating realm of prophetic revelation. The places the prophet travels or sees into, the spiritual realms, are outside of the natural, visual, time and sound spectrum.[26] The Holy Spirit provides the prophet with the ability to enter His realm of spiritual intimacy and worship.

A prophet receives commandments, prophecies and revelations from God; he is responsible for making known God's will and God's true character to mankind. He denounces sin and foretells its consequences. His primary responsibility is to bear witness of Christ. In Numbers 12:6 KJV it states, *"And he said, Hear now my words: if there be a prophet among you, I the LORD will make myself known unto him in a vision, and will speak unto him in a dream."*

Because we are students of the bible, we also understand that the church is built on a foundation of Apostles and Prophets with Jesus Christ being the Chief Cornerstone (Eph. 2:20). Subsequently, we obey the Word of the Lord which says to quench not the Spirit and despise not prophesying (1 Thess. 5:19-20). Now that we receive God's prophet, allow us to be taught on the power of God's prophet.

The power of God lies in the power of the

Prophet. 1 Kings 17:1 KJV corroborates this fact, "And Elijah the Tishbite, of the inhabitants of Gilead, said to Ahab, As the LORD God of Israel lives, before whom I stand, there shall not be dew or rain these years, except at my word." The bibles tells us that it occurred just as Elijah spoke it- the power of the prophet!

Elijah performed numerous miracles, signs and wonders. It was he who called down fire to prove Jehovah is the Only True and Living God when he tested the god of Baal. The prophet has the ability to alter climate conditions. The power of the prophet is designed to resurrect dead issues in: individuals, communities, nations, churches, governments and the world. Life and death lies in the power of the prophet's tongue. He has the power to speak prosperity and favor and death; he has the power to speak overflow or drought and famine; he has the power to speak blessings or call down curses. The prophetic power within the prophet can cause generational blessings to be provoked and generational curses to be forfeited. The prophet exhibits the *dunamis* power of God!

He can pray and change the verdict of God. His specialty is to resurrect dead issues on every hand. The prophet is exemplary of Deuteronomy 28:10 KJV, "And all people of the earth shall see that you are called by the Name of the LORD: and they shall be afraid of you." Here lies the POWER of the prophet!

HOW TO DOMINATE THE PROPHETIC REALM

CHAPTER 7

THE BENEFITS OF THE PROPHET

Now that we understand and concur with the fact that great power lies in that of the Prophet, we shall move forward to learning the emphatic benefits of having a prophet in our lives. In Matthew 10:41 NKJV it states, "He who receives a prophet in the name of a prophet shall receive a prophet's reward. And he who receives a righteous man in the name of a righteous man shall receive a righteous man's reward." **THERE ARE GREAT BENEFITS IN RECEIVING A PROPHET IN**

THE NAME OF A PROPHET. The bible tells us
when we receive a prophet in the name of
a prophet we **receive the reward due to the
prophet.** Thus, we receive a prophet's reward.
So, what is a prophet's reward? When we
receive it what are we actually receiving?
Allow me the opportunity to share.

The word "receive" is defined by Merriam-
Webster as "to take into one's possession."[27]
The word "receive" is synonymous to the
words: accept, acquire, be given, be told,
catch, collect, hear, grab, hold, inherit, take
possession.[28] Therefore, when we accept, hold,
hear and take possession of a prophet in the
authoritative name of a prophet, we SHALL
SEE RESULTS!

Some <u>benefits</u> of obtaining a prophet's
Reward include:

> **That which cannot be purchased-
> that which cannot be bought**
> **The gift of the desire of the heart
> that only God can grant**

When you receive a prophet you take in the

prophetic word being spoken and you
recognize it is the Voice of God telling
the prophet what to speak. You acknowledge
the prophetic gift and receive the ministry of
the prophet as it is fulfilled according to the
Word of the Lord. In receiving a prophet, your
Spirit unites with the prophecy, you obey
God's Word and you receive a prophet's
reward. The American Dictionary defines
reward as "something given or received in
recompense for worthy behavior."[29]
Therefore, a prophet's reward includes, but
is not limited to, the following:

**A. Having The Prophet Tell God To
Meet Your Need Now**- The example
for us is Numbers 12:13 KJV where
Moses, God's prophet, cried out to the
Lord on Miriam's behalf after she
offended the Lord by stirring up anger
against Moses when he married an
Ethiopian woman. The Lord blatantly
told Aaron and Miriam that He spoke

directly to Moses-face to face- yet they were NOT afraid to speak against HIS servant Moses. **Because of the prophet**, Miriam was relieved of the leprosy placed on her body as a result of the direct sin against the Lord.

B. **Miracles: Turning Tragedies into Triumph-**Here we see in 1 Kings 17: 17-24 NKJV that Elijah, who prophesied to the widow woman that sustained him during the drought he caused had a severe tragedy- her only son died. She asked Elijah if he came to judge her for her sins and kill her boy. Elijah, moved with compassion, took the lifeless boy and carried him to the upper room where he was staying while with the widow. Elijah laid the boy on the bed then cried out to the Lord. Let's visit verses 20-21 NKJV, "Then he cried out to the LORD and said, **O LORD my God**, have You also brought tragedy on t he widow with whom I lodge, by killing h er son? **And he stretched himself out on the child three times, and cried out to the LORD and said, O LORD my God, I pray, let this child's soul come back to him."** In verses 22-24 NKJV it states, "Then the LORD **heard the voice of Elijah**; and the soul of the child came back to him, and he revived. And Elijah took the child and brought him down from the upper room into the house, and gave him to his mother. And Elijah said, See, your son lives! Then the woman said to Elijah, now by this I know that you are a man of God, and that the word of the LORD in your mouth is the truth."

C. **Getting Secrets From God And Knowing The Heart Of God Towards You-** Let us look at Amos 3:7 NKJV, "Surely the Lord GOD does nothing, unless He reveals His secret to His servants the prophets." God's true prophets, His servants, have God's secret abiding with them; this comes directly from the heart of God. As a result they can reveal these to you.

D. **Obtaining Increase and Favor-** Our example here will be taken from 2 Chronicles 20:20 NKJV. Jehoshaphat stood and said to the people, "Hear me, O Judah and you inhabitants of Jerusalem: Believe in the LORD your God, and you shall be established; believe His prophets, and you shall prosper." Here, we see DIRECTLY in the Word of God that **IF WE BELIEVE GOD'S PROPHETS we shall prosper.**

E. **Obtaining Blessings-**This benefit can be effectively corroborated in Numbers 23:19-20 NKJV. Here, the LORD put a Word in Balaam's mouth. Balak asked the prophet to curse the people, but the Lord commanded a blessing by telling the prophet to bless the people and by COMMANDING a blessing out of the mouth of the prophet. In verse 19-20, we see, "God is not a man, that He should lie, nor a son of man, that He should repent. Has He said, and will He not do? Or has He spoken, and will He not make it good? Behold, I have received a **COMMAND** to bless; **He has blessed and I cannot reverse it."**

F. Obtaining Divine Direction, Wisdom and Revelation- This next benefit can allow you the ability to sustain your life and/or to lose it. In Ecclesiastes it states "Why should you die before your time?" (Ecc. 7:17 NKJV). The bible clearly tells us we can die prematurely. Listening to the prophet allows divine direction, God's wisdom and His revelation which gives us a plethora of blessings and benefits. Our example will be taken from 2 Kings 9: 1-13 NKJV, and it states, *And Elisha the* prophet called one of the sons of the prophets, and said to him, "Get yourself ready, take this flask of oil in your hand, and go to Ramoth Gilead. Now when you arrive at that place, look there for Jehu the son of Jehoshaphat, the son of Nimshi, and go in and make him rise up from among his associates, and take him to an inner room. Then take the flask of oil, and pour it on his head, and say, Thus says the LORD: I have anointed you king over Israel. Then open the door and flee, and do not delay." So the young man, the servant of the prophet, went to Ramoth Gilead. And when he arrived, there were the captains of the army sitting; and he said, "I have a message for you, Commander." Jehu said, "For which one of us?" And he said, "For you, Commander." Then he arose and went into the house. And he poured the oil on his head, and said to him, "Thus *says the LORD God of Israel: 'I have anointed you king over the people of the LORD, over Israel. You shall strike down the house of Ahab your master, that I may avenge the blood of My servants the prophets, and the blood of all the servants of the LORD, at the hand of Jezebel. For the whole house of Ahab shall perish; and I will cut off from Ahab all the males in Israel, both bond and free . So I will make the house of Ahab like the house of Jeroboam the son of Nebat, and like the house of Baasha the son of Ahijah. The dogs shall eat Jezebel on the plot of ground at Jezreel, and there shall be none to bury her.'"*

And he opened the door and fled. Then came out to the servants of his master, and one said to him, "Is all well? Why did this madman come to you?" And he said to them, "You know the man and his babble." And they said, "A lie! Tell us now." So he said, "Thus and thus he spoke to me, saying, 'Thus says the LORD: I have anointed you king over Israel.'" Then each man hastened to take his garment and put it under him on the top of the steps; and they blew trumpets, saying, "Jehu is king!" So here we see this passage of scripture has very important revelations and lessons. First, Elisha called one of the sons of the prophets to deliver God's message. Next, this son had to provide his undivided attention to this task and execute it with clarity and precision. Why do you think this had to b e so? The answer is his very LIFE depended on him paying attention to detail. Next, he had to follow the EXACT direction, go to the exact place, and say the EXACT Words given to him. This is a very good example of **divine direction, wisdom and revelation**. The son journeyed to the exact place

and found his scenario just as the
Prophet Elisha had said. Next, he took
Jehu inside in private and spoke the
Word of the LORD to Jehu. Notice, God
came upon the son and gave him more
to speak than what Elisha had said.
After he performed his task, he fled
expediently for his safety. This son took
a chance standing in the company of the
commanders. Any opposition to these
renowned leaders would result in his
death. Also, those words spoken in
the ear of the wrong person could have
meant death. This was a very grave
responsibility but God knew just who to
send. The task was explicitly followed,
accurately carried out, and successfully
completed allowing the son to live and
God's will to be done. I am sure there
were more benefits for this son when he
returned and as he grew in the gift of
the prophetic. God rewards our faith and

faithfulness.

**G. Having Your Little Become More
Than Enough-** We will revisit the
widow in 1 Kings 17:13-16 NKJV,
And Elijah said to her, "Do not fear; go
and do as you have said, but make me
a small cake from it first, and bring it to
me; and afterward make some for
yourself and your son. For thus says
the LORD God of Israel: the bin of flour s
hall not be used up, nor shall the jar of o
il run dry, until the day the LORD
sends rain on the earth." So she went
away and did according to the word of
Elijah; and she and he and her
household ate for many days. The bin
of flour was not used up, nor did the jar
of oil run dry, according to the word of
the LORD which He spoke by Elijah. I
get excited about Elijah because many
have spoken prophetic words to me
that the LORD has called me a "Modern
Day Elijah." It is the Word of the Lord

and it is so! Now, when this story began
the widow woman, who had lost her
sole source of provisions, her husband,
was preparing for the death of her son
and her. She was not from the promised
land, but she was from Jezebel's
territory (the enemy of Elijah).
Anyway, her heritage was the practice
of polytheism- worshipping many or
more than one god. However, she knew
of Elijah and she knew of his GREAT
GOD JEHOVAH! Because she followed
the Word of the LORD out of the
Prophet's mouth her entire household
as well as God's prophet was sustained.
Allow me to interject here. It is sad that
so many people suffer because they are
fearful and full of doubt when the Lord
God and His servant the Prophet are
collectively trying to bless them instead
of have them continue in lack, bondage,
agony, pain and derision. **The prophet**

does NOT desire to take from you. We MUST remember that he/she represents God. God does NOT desire to hurt you in ANY way; His inherent desire is TO BLESS YOU! One must receive every matter from the prophet as LIFE or DEATH because it is just that important to God. Because of the **obedience** of the widow woman; **TOTAL** obedience, she lived a long and prosperous life when death was supposed to be her portion. God is awesome!

H. **Power To Intervene-** Another benefit is the power of the prophet to intervene on God's peoples' behalf. Let us look at Numbers 11:1-2 NKJV. It states, *Now when the people complained, it displeased the LORD; for the LORD heard it, and His anger was aroused. So the fire of the LORD burned among them, and consumed some in the outskirts of the camp. Then* *the people cried out to Moses, and when Moses prayed to the LORD, the fire was quenched.* The prophet is as a "Moses" to God's people. He/she can consult with God on the peoples' behalf and have God give him/her his desire. It is ONLY when we walk in true covenant with God that this can occur.

HOW TO DOMINATE THE PROPHETIC REALM

CHAPTER 8

THE DANGER IN JUDGING
THE PROPHET

"The Lord thy God will raise up unto thee a Prophet from the midst of thee, of thy brethren, like unto me; unto him ye shall hearken," (Deut. 18:15 KJV).

"I will raise them up a Prophet from among their brethren, like unto thee, and I will put my words in his mouth;

and he shall speak unto them all that I shall command him," (Deut. 18:18 KJV).

"And it shall come to pass, that whosoever will not hearken unto my words which **he shall speak** in my Name, I will REQUIRE it of him," (Deut. 18:19 KJV).

"And if thou say in thine heart, How shall we know the word which the LORD has spoken? When a prophet speaketh in the name of the LORD, if the thing follow not, nor come to pass, that is the thing which the LORD hath not spoken but the prophet hath spoken it presumptuously: thou shalt not be afraid of him," (Deut. 18:21-22 KJV).

A prophet has a VERY SEVERE and awesome responsibility to give the Word of the LORD; this is not a game and

should not be taken lightly. God honors
His prophet because the assignment of
the prophet is to die to self--- fears,
doubts and excuses--- and drink the cup
of suffering that accompanies the
genuine call of God. The power of life
and death exists in the tongue, as we
have already elaborated on, especially
regarding the prophetic Word from God.
For the prophet, being used in the
prophetic is sometimes an excessive
and painful issue and his/her
obedience costs. No matter what---
the prophet MUST obey God. Many
prophets have been killed in reference
to this phenomenon.

When given a prophetic word,
we must remember to weigh the word
and not to judge the giver of the word.
We must ask the Lord for wisdom in how
to receive, interpret or apply the word
given to us, or if we are to receive the

word at all. Every word must be tested regardless of the reputation of the prophetic voice giving it. A true prophet will not be insulted; he or she will rejoice that you are obeying the command in scripture to test the Word. We know the Word of the Lord that comes out of the prophet's mouth carries with it:

➢ **God's Truth**
➢ **God's Power**
➢ **God's Authority**

Therefore, it is extremely imperative that a person does not judge, condemn or "put his/her mouth on" the prophet of God. Psalm 105:15 KJV states, "Saying, touch not my anointed, and do my prophets no harm." Here, God admonishes and forewarns people about causing any harm to His prophets. A prophet is known throughout the earth, because God establishes him or her. God specifically said all people of the earth SHALL SEE that His prophets are called by the Name of the LORD; and they shall be afraid of them. Let me just reiterate the fact that life and death lie in the power of God's prophets' tongues.

Remember Elisha in the book of 2 Kings 2:23-24 KJV, *"And he went up from thence unto Bethel: and as he was going up by the way, there came forth little children out of the city, and mocked him, and said unto him, Go up thou bald head; go up, thou bald head. And he turned back, and looked on them, and cursed them in the name of the LORD. And there came forth two she bears out of the wood, and tare forty and two children of them."*

Here is a prime example of the results of judging the prophet. These disrespectful youths angered the prophet and he cursed them in the

Name of the LORD. They were mauled. The God-ordained power in the tongue of God's chosen, selected, hand-picked servant is dynamic- *dunamis*! God has killed many people because they judged His servant, His prophet.

Remember Moses, Aaron, Miriam and their story in Numbers 12: 1-16 KJV. Aaron and Miriam judged Moses because he chose to marry an Ethiopian woman. Moses was faithful and meek, and the LORD came and punished Miriam and Aaron. Miriam was struck with leprosy for seven (7) days.

God asked them that seeing they knew the profound relationship between the LORD and Moses, how were they **NOT AFRAID** to speak against Moses? When you offend God's prophet not only is the man of God able to curse you even unto death, but God will avenge His man. God has corroborated and given examples of this TRUTH in His Holy Writ

time and time again. In Genesis 12:3
God tells Abram that He will bless those
who bless him and curse him who curses
Abram. In Isaiah 43:13 KJV it states,
"Yea, before the day was I am He; and
there is none that can deliver out of My
Hand: I will work, and who shall let it?"
God is so Mighty that He boasts that no
one can deliver anyone who He decides
to put in His Hand. When God curses,
no man can bless, and when God
blesses, no man can curse!

Many times our blessings are held
up because we have placed our mouth
on God's people. We must **watch what
we speak** because God warns us that
every idle word that men shall speak
they MUST give an account before God.
We will be justified or condemned by
our very own words.

We must remember that our tongue
is a fire; it is a world of iniquity. Our

tongue, despite the fact that it is a little member, defiles the whole body. No man can tame the tongue; it is an unruly evil, full of deadly poison. People bless God with the tongue, and use the exact same tongue to curse men who are made in God's image and likeness. Blessings and cursing should not proceed out of the same mouth.

Another mishap in judging the prophet entails not obeying God's prophet. Let us take a look in the book of 2 Kings 5:27 KJV, "The leprosy therefore of Naaman shall cleave unto thee, and unto thy seed forever. And he (Gehazi) went out from his (Elisha, the prophet's) presence a leper as white as snow." It is with great caution that I admonish you, as God's servant, **not to lie** to a prophet or **blatantly disobey** God's prophet(ess). The prophet is no ordinary man; the Spirit of God is with the Spirit of the Man of God. Therefore, lying and disobedience will cause catastrophic results. Here, in the Old Testament, Gehazi thought he would ingeniously go behind the prophet's back and ask Naaman for recompense using some lame excuse that two young men of the sons of the prophets had come down to visit and required some things, AND that his master had sent him. Not only was Gehazi lying, but he was lying in the name of the prophet, his MASTER.

Imagine lying on your boss; or even more seriously, lying on God or lying in the Name of God. People do this every day, but that is why their lives have chaos; that is the reason their loved ones cannot get delivered; that is the reason they lose their mind; go to jail or even get killed or come up dead or with some deadly illness. We must remember how serious lying is and how serious and severe is speaking death on others with our mouths, especially if it is God's prophets.

The bible declares obedience is better than ANY sacrifice one can give. So if you had to choose to obey God or offer God a sacrifice, God would rather you OBEY HIM! He does not need or have to accept your sacrifice. God, through His Word, informs us that rebellion, which is disobedience, is as the sin of witchcraft. He tells us stubbornness is as iniquity and idolatry. This is TOTAL rejection towards God when a person decides to lie, rebel or be stubborn against the words of God's prophet. God says in 1 Samuel 15:23 KJV that because Saul rejected the words of the prophet (hence he rejected God Himself), God tells Saul He has rejected him from being king from that very moment. Think of this for a moment do you REALLY want God to reject you? We are speaking of God, the Great God Jehovah; the One Who IS and WAS and IS TO COME; we are speaking of Master Jehovah-The Sovereign One; the Creator of Heaven and Earth; the Elohim Who is in Covenant relationship with His people. Now, do you really want to reject God and have God reject you? I am sure your answer is "no." Subsequently, we must be mindful when speaking about God's people, especially when we may be in danger of using words that judge God's prophet(ess).

The bible tells us not to judge, so that God will not judge us. Let us look at Matthew 7:1-5 NKJV. It says, "Judge n ot, that you be not judged. For with what judgment you judge, you will be judged; and with the measure you use, it will be measured back to you. And

why do you look at the speck in your
brother's eye, but do not consider the
plank in your own eye? Or how can you
say to your brother, 'Let me remove
the speck from your eye; and look, a
plank is in your own eye?' Hypocrite!
First remove the plank from your own
eye, and then you will see clearly to
remove the speck from your brother's
eye." God admonishes us about judging
our brothers, so how much more His
prophets? We must refrain from
speaking ill against God's chosen
servants, the prophets.

CHAPTER 9

THE SPIRIT OF THE PROPHET

In serving a prophet and/or being directly under the headship or leadership of a prophet, we must know and understand that the prophet's Spirit is with us. 1 Corinthians 14:32 KJV states, "And the spirits of the prophets are subject to the prophets." This means anyone who disobeys the prophet or acts disorderly in the name of the Holy

143

Spirit is out of order with God. Some
people say that the Holy Spirit is moving
on them and they must interrupt or
make a loud outburst in the middle of
a service or orderly meeting, but this is n
ot God or His Spirit, because God is not
the author of confusion but of peace.
Also, the Word of God says to do all
things decently, in decency and in
order. God never goes against His Word.

Another factor of being undergirded
by a prophet is that we are to realize
that the testimony of Jesus is the spirit
of prophecy. Prophecy and the Spirit
behind it testifies that Jesus is Lord.
Therefore, the prophet MUST align
his/her life through the Holy Spirit,
with the Word of God. Man is NOT
perfect, and the prophet is a man or
woman, so they will never be perfect.
However, their lives must align with
the unadulterated Word of God. There
are MANY false prophets with ulterior

motives in the world today, so we must KNOW the Word of God in order to keep ourselves from other men's sins according to the bible.

A true prophet will never try to steal God's glory and act as if he/she is the force behind the healings or blessings provided to God's people. It is t he power of God working on the inside of them that allows these miracles, signs and wonders to occur. We know and understand that these are solely caused by God. The Lord will show mercy to whom He will show mercy, and He will have favor on whom He desires to show favor toward. It is exclusively God's choice, yet remember, a true prophet can alter God's decision!

Now, let us go into detail about the Spirit of the prophet. We will use Gehazi as our first example. Elisha had Gehazi as his servant. Let me interject the fact that if you are directly serving a prophet, then his/her spirit is with you. Gehazi should have already known that Elisha's spirit travels with him just as my spirit travels with many of my sons and daughters. As a servant, one should never endeavor to override what his leader says. When Elisha said he wanted nothing from Naaman it was settled.

Please never allow the enemy to enter your heart and allow you to be used by him as Gehazi did. First of all he had nothing to do with the miracle. Secondly, he represented his master, and the bible says no servant is greater than his master. Thirdly, he took advantage of his master's good deeds and tried to use these to get selfish gain. The master had the responsibility of taking care of the servant, so his needs were met.

In 2 Kings 5:25 KJV is states, "But he (Gehazi) went in, and stood before his master (Elisha). And Elisha said unto him, Whence comest thou, Gehazi? And he said, Thy servant went no whither." Verse 26 KJV says, "And he said unto him, Went not mine heart with thee, when the man turned again from his chariot to meet thee? Is it a time to receive money, and to receive garments, and oliveyards, and vineyards, and sheep, and oxen, and menservants, and maidservants?" So, Elisha not only was well aware of what Gehazi had done, but he knew the plan Gehazi had in his heart. Because of all the things Elisha mentioned above in verse 26 in the curse on Gehazi, Elisha saw his heart and knew Gehazi had plans to spend those 2 talents of silver, which was approximately $3,840, on the things Elisha mentioned. Well, Gehazi was given the short end of the deal,

because he was cursed, his family was
cursed and he left the presence of the
prophet. That reminds me of the time
Adam and Eve had to leave the
presence of God. Also, Cain had to
go from the presence of the Lord. Is
ANYTHING worth your ability to be
in the presence of the Lord? What is
in earth that you would desire enough
to trade being in God's presence for it?

Allow us to look at another example
regarding the spirit of the prophet. Let
us look at Naomi and Ruth. These
two women, mother-in-law and
daughter-in-law had to return to
Naomi's homeland from Moab because
the Lord had blessed His people in
the land of Judah, and there was a
famine in Moab. Naomi acted as a
prophetess to Ruth in directing her to
gain a kinsman redeemer to wed her.
Ruth entrusted Naomi with her life and
Her destiny; therefore Ruth was married

By her husband's family redeemer.

Because Ruth had resided with Naomi for so long, Ruth took on the spirit of Naomi as opposed to her Moabite beliefs of polytheism. Ruth received Jehovah, Naomi's God, as her own and because of this fact, God redeemed Ruth. Not only did Ruth gain a husband, but she obtained her own book in the bible as well as became a part of the direct lineage of Jesus in having Obed, her son. The spirit of the prophet is transferrable and it allows for miraculous results in the lives of people with hopeless or helpless situations. If Ruth would not have obeyed everything that Naomi told her to do, she would have missed out on her deliverance and her lineage of blessings.

The spirit of the prophet is not only transferrable, but servants who are passionate enough, who possess pure motives, and who God chooses can obtain a double portion of the prophet's anointing/ spirit. 2 Kings 2:9-10 KJV states, *"And it came to pass, when they were gone over, that Elijah said unto Elisha, Ask what I shall do for thee, before I be taken away from thee. And Elisha said, I pray thee, let a double portion of thy spirit be upon me. And he said, Thou hast asked a hard thing: nevertheless, if thou see me when I am taken from thee, it shall be so unto thee; but if not, it shall not be so."*

Here, we see that Elisha has asked that he gain a double portion of Elijah's spirit. There are different measures of the Holy Spirit and power that men have received, and our example here shows us this fact. Also, Elijah made it known to Elisha that this was a hard thing to obtain. How could a man impart twice as much anointing as he himself had?

The answer is he could not without God.
Elijah could only accomplish this by
faith and by having Jehovah honoring
Elijah's request to provide a double
portion for Elisha. God allowed it!

Elisha asked a very hard thing;
he would have to fulfill what it meant
to obtain a double portion, and that
was to walk double the way Elijah
walked. As a result of his double
portion, Elisha performed miracles
that doubled the amount of Elijah!

As we continue to enter God's
higher realms and tap into the
prophetic in a more intense manner,
we will master the domination of the
prophetic. This will allow God to use
each and every one of us and assist
in His plan of building His Kingdom.
Next, we will expound on the spirit of
the prophet in a significant and
substantial and manner. Please join

HOW TO DOMINATE THE PROPHETIC REALM

us in the next exposition.

ANTOINE M. JASMINE

ABOUT THE AUTHOR

Prophet Antoine Michael Jasmine answered the call of God to be a Prophet at age 16. He fell "head over heels" in love with God as a young, shy teen. His gift was corroborated through the laying on of hands by the presbytery. The elders decreed that he would be a prophet to the nations. Little d id the young prophet know that he would spend the rest of his life interpreting dreams and tongues, having dreams, visions and visitations from God. He vowed allegiance to God and never looked back!

Today, Prophet Antoine Jasmine is the General Overseer of Choice International Ministries, one church in two locations, LaPlace, Louisiana and Dayton, Ohio. He is also the founder and/or overseer of Choice Music Academy, Andwar Publishing Company, and Choice Entertainment Company. Although he is a Pastor and he is very serious about fulfilling his pastoral assignment, God has commissioned him to

153

own, spearhead and oversee a multiplicity of businesses, corporations, community development programs and much, much more. God has called Prophet Jasmine to expose this generation of believers to another level of life by following the blueprint provided in Matthew 28:19. Because of the Word of God, Prophet Jasmine selflessly uses his personal ministerial experiences that God allows him to encounter to alter the mindsets of this generation of believers.

Prophet Jasmine believes in going forth preaching the unadulterated Gospel of Jesus Christ, while preaching, teaching and ministering under the anointing of the Holy Spirit with evidence of healings, miracles, signs and wonders just as Jesus did and commissioned us to do. He believes the Gospel is not limited to just the church and to Jesus alone, but it is a lso inclusive of the concepts, principles, and philosophies of life that help advance and alter the consciousness of this generation. Prophet Jasmines allows all to know that they do not have to conform to the expectations of society; they are crafted by God to do exceeding, abundantly above all they can ask or think in whatever arena of life they desire.

One profound, life-altering experience that Prophet Jasmine shares is the way God used him to restore his once dysfunctional family, introduce the entire family to God, and redirect relationships. His parents were divorced while he was in college, yet God miraculously used Prophet Jasmine and his ministry to reunite his parents with the honor of having him marry them this time. Today, his entire family serves alongside him at Choice International Ministries. Prophet Antoine Jasmine is God's Man; he is the hub of versatility and strength for other prophets, his ministry and the world.

REFERENCES

1. abomination. (n.d.). *Collins English Dictionary – Complete & Unabridged 10th Edition*. Retrieved October 02, 2013, from Dictionary.com website: http://dictionary.reference.com/browse/abomination

2. Dake,F.(2001).Dake's Annotated Reference Bible-The Holy Bible. Lawrenceville: Dake Publishing, Inc.

3. Dake,F.(2001).Dake's Annotated Reference Bible-The Holy Bible. Lawrenceville: Dake Publishing, Inc.

4. Dake,F.(2001).Dake's Annotated Reference Bible-The Holy Bible. Lawrenceville: Dake Publishing, Inc.

5. "The Meaning of 9" retrieved from, http://www.biblestudy.org/bibleref/meaning-of-numbers-in-bible/9.html

6. carnality. (n.d.). *Easton's 1897 Bible Dictionary*. Retrieved October 03, 2013, from Dictionary.com website: http://dictionary.reference.com/browse/carnality

7. Rambally.R.(n.d.).Prophetic Warfare Breakth

rough Prayer Ministries. Prophet/Prophetess. retrieved 8-13-13 from; http://www.rohanra mbally.org/Resources.htm

8. Rambally.R.(n.d.).Prophetic Warfare Breakth rough Prayer Ministries. Prophet/Prophetess. retrieved 8-13-13 from; http://www.rohanra mbally.org/Resources.htm

9. Wallis, S.(2011).Deeper Prophetic Realms. Retrieved 8-14-14 from: http://www.prophe tcentral.com/2011/11/deeper-prophetic-real ms.html

10. realm. (n.d.). *Dictionary.com Unabridged.* Re- trieved October 03, 2013, from Dictionary.com website: http://dictionary.refer- ence.com/browse/realm

11. Pond, R.(2010). Season of Peace.Freedom Fr om Fear-Seeing With Spiritual Eyes. Retrieve d 8-19-13 from: http//season.org/freedom-f rom-fear-seeing-with-spiritual-eyes/

12. Dake,F.(2001).Dake's Annotated Reference

Bible-The Holy Bible. Lawrenceville: Dake
Publishing, Inc.

13. Realms of Prophetic Gifts. Retrieved Septem
ber 15,2013 from: http://www.docstoc.com/
docs/420977744/Realms0Of-PROPHETIC-GI
FTS

14. dominion. (n.d.). *Dictionary.com Unabridged*.
Retrieved October 03, 2013, from Diction-
ary.com website: http://dictionary.refer-
ence.com/browse/dominion

15. Dake,F.(2001).Dake's Annotated Reference
Bible-The Holy Bible. Lawrenceville: Dake
Publishing, Inc.

16. Revelation.(n.d). WordIQ.com. Retrieved 9-
5-13, from http://www.wordiq.com/definitio
n/Revelation

17. Wayne, D.(n.d.).The Prophetic View- Unders
tanding Prophetic. Retrieved 8-12-13, from:
http://www.thepropheticview.com/understa
ndingprophetic.htm

18. Got Questions?org.(2013).What is Zion? Wh
at is Mount Zion? Retrieved 8-13-13 from: h

ttp://www.gotquestions.org/Printer/Zion-PF.html

19. Dake,F.(2001).Dake's Annotated Reference Bible-The Holy Bible. Lawrenceville: Dake Publishing, Inc.

20. Stewart, D.(n.d.).Mysteries In The Word of God. Retrieved 9-6-2013 from: http://www.jesus-is-savior.com/Believer%27%s%20Corner/Doctrines/mysteries.htm

21. Dake,F.(2001).Dake's Annotated Reference Bible-The Holy Bible. Lawrenceville: Dake Publishing, Inc.

22. Dake,F.(2001).Dake's Annotated Reference Bible-The Holy Bible. Lawrenceville: Dake Publishing, Inc.

23. Branam, L.(n.d.).Sermon: Paul's Visit to Paradise. Retrieved 9-9-13 from: http://sanfernandochurchofchrist.com/SermonView.aspx?ID=800

24. engrossed. (n.d.). *Dictionary.com Unabridged.* Retrieved October 03, 2013, from Diction- ary.com website: http://dictionary.refer- ence.com/browse/engrossed

25. Peters-Colley, D.(n.d). The Prophet's Reward FREE STUDY. Retrieved 9-13-13 from, http: //www.seaministries.net/page31a.html

26. Paul, K.(n.d.) Ezine Articles. Prophetic- The Power of the prophetic Seer. Retrieved 9-13- 13, from http://ezinearticles.com/?prophetic ---The-Power-of-the-Prophetic-Seer&id=805 807

27. "Receive." *Merriam-Webster.com.* Merriam-Webste r,(n.d). Web. 4 Oct. 2013. <http://www.merriam-we bster.com/dictionary/receive>.

28. receive. (n.d.). *Roget's 21st Century Thesau- rus, Third Edition.* Retrieved October 03, 2013, from Thesaurus.com website: http://thesau- rus.com/browse/receive

29. reward. (n.d.). *Collins English Dictionary - Complete & Unabridged 10th Edition.* Re- trieved October 03, 2013, from Dictionary.com website: http://dictionary.refer- ence.com/browse/reward

ANTOINE M. JASMINE

PRODUCTS AND SERVICES

Prophet Antoine Jasmine can be reached for
speaking engagements via www.choiceim.com
and (985) 651-7844. Also, you may purchase
his sermons, products and Blessed Anointed
Oils on the website. If you believe you are
called by God into the prophetic, feel free
to sign up for Prophet Jasmine's School
of the Prophets. For more information please
visit Prophet Jasmine on You-Tube type in
Prophet A. Jasmine; Facebook search
Prophet A. Jasmine; Twitter- type in
@ProphetAJasmine and on our website at
www.choiceim.com; you may also follow
Prophet Jasmine via live streaming every
Wednesday at 7pm CST and every Saturday
at 11:45am CST at www.rightchoicetv.com.

HOW TO DOMINATE THE PROPHETIC REALM

Made in the USA
San Bernardino, CA
04 May 2016